I Believe in Man

by

GEORGE CAREY

WILLIAM B. EERDMANS PUBLISHING COMPANY

Library of Congress Cataloging in Publication Data

Carey, George.
 I believe in man.

 Includes index.
  1. Man (Christian theology)   I.   Title.
BT701.2.C295   233   77-13426
ISBN 0-8028-1711-4

Editor's Preface

It might at first sight seem a curious thing to find a title like *I Believe in Man* in a series which sets out to reconsider central Christian doctrines in the light both of the Scriptures and of contemporary experience. But a moment's reflection suggests that the subject of man (who is he? what is his nature, his destiny?) is perhaps the world's central issue: it is certain to dominate the remainder of the twentieth century. No understanding of Christian doctrine can hope to be either relevant or complete without giving serious attention to the doctrine of man. What is more, the Bible encourages us to do just this. Man is as much the subject matter of the Bible as is God. Man is seen as God's vice-gerent on earth, made a little lower than the angels in order to display both sovereignty over God's world and loyalty to God's suzerainty. Man's dominance over the environment is taken for granted today. But we do not take God's claims upon us at all seriously. To a society of self-made men, confident of our technological competence, nourished on the dream of progress, the very idea of God is faintly absurd, and completely irrelevant.

Or is it? We certainly have enormous problems, in the realms of ecology, abortion, euthanasia, biological engineering, class and race, international and industrial relationships, the place of man and woman, the increase of crime, the breakdown of societal ties. What if God is not a convenient myth made in our image? What if man is made in His? What if we have been leaving out of consideration the crucial factor in all our human problems — the God dimension?

These are matters of the highest significance for the human race. And George Carey has tackled the main ones head on in this, his first book. It is an enormous undertaking to attempt an analysis and an evaluation of man. The breadth of knowledge required is daunting in the extreme. Dr. Carey has not shrunk from facing the cardinal issues in a proper understanding of man, and he has brought to them a considerable breadth both of knowledge and experience. He is no ivory-tower theologian. Indeed, he left school at 14 without any academic qualifications at all. Shortly afterwards he discovered in his own experience the power of the Creator to remake a life that is surrendered to him. He became a Christian. Almost at once he found his intellectual interests and accomplishments expanding. He taught himself subjects like French while on National Service. He gained O and A levels, entered theological college, and began to train for the ordained ministry. He not only became a most useful and valued pastor, but gained a good London B.D. degree, and followed it up with a Master's degree and a doctorate. He has taught Christian doctrine in two theological colleges, and I know from first hand experience how his care and friendship have warmed both staff and students, while his thinking and teaching have stretched them. He is now engaged in a significant parish ministry in the heart of Durham, working both among the City and the student congregation.

I am delighted that in the course of a busy life he has been able to make time to write this book, and I commend it warmly.

MICHAEL GREEN

Foreword

Anyone who writes a book on the subject of man does so with a little hesitation and trepidation. The reason is twofold. First of all not only is, this a vast subject taking in such disciplines as anthropology, psychology, sociology and many other related branches of knowledge, but all the time fresh literature is appearing which alters our knowledge a little here and a little there. Man, it seems, cannot stop writing about himself! While this indicates the relevance of the subject, it serves also as a painful reminder that it is quite impossible for a writer to be comprehensive. Secondly, and this time from a distinctly Christian point of view, the doctrine of man is more a nexus of doctrines than a doctrine in its own right. It cannot be isolated from other topics. Think of man and before we know where we are we are talking about God, Christ, salvation, the Church and so on. We are warned by this fact that the subject will take us far afield and we shall have to wander here and there seeking this creature who is a mystery to himself.

In spite of the literature available on our topic, the problem of man comes before us with renewed urgency. While there is much in human existence that is good, wholesome and healthy, and there is a great deal in man's achievements to warrant confidence, we have to face the fact that deep pessimism regarding man is common in Western society. Modern man does not know what to believe about himself, or how to resolve the contradictions within, or how to live at peace with others. This pessimism contrasts sharply with the Christian perspective which says, 'Yes, we believe in man. We believe that this creature though spoiled by sin may be renewed through Christ and have a glorious future because he is made in the likeness of God.' The aim of this volume then, is to explore some of the issues relating to man, his relationships and his life as a human being, from a Christian perspective.

I would like to express my thanks for all those who have taught me more of what it means to be a truly human person. To Michael Green, a dear friend and colleague for many years; to my former colleagues on the staff of St. John's College, Nottingham; and, of course, to many students of St. John's with whom I have had so much fun, which is, when all is said and done, part of this business of being human! And where would I be without my wife Eileen...?

Finally, my grateful thanks to all my friends who assisted me in the preparation of this book. To Anne, Janet, Joy and Joyce who deciphered my writing and typed the manuscript. Thanks are also due to Mrs. Rosemary Jackson, Dr. Ernie Ashcroft, Mr. Stephen Morris, the Ven. Michael Perry, and especially the Rev. John Williams who read the manuscript and made many helpful criticisms and suggestions.

Above all I thank the good Lord who time and again has proved the reality of the power to make us 'new creatures'.

GEORGE CAREY

Contents

CHAPTER 1

Man — Nature's Riddle?

MODERN MAN'S DIFFICULTIES with Christianity come not so much from its teaching about God as from its assumed doctrine of man. From his schooldays on, the average civilised person is introduced to a picture of man which Niebuhr expresses as 'that of a little animal living a precarious existence on a second-rate planet, attached to a second-rate sun'.[1] Such a statement appears to be a reasonable inference from modern biological research together with our growing knowledge of the universe. The evolutionary theory of man's ascent from lower forms of life is the lynch-pin of modern anthropology. No longer unique in creation, he is considered to be the product of an ever broadening stream of life which began as a trickle some 2,000 million years ago. Hector Hawton, a humanist thinker once stated, '300 million years ago my ancestor was a fish.' We can no longer think of our planet as particularly exceptional. Copernicus may have been the first to question the centrality of planet earth in the solar system, but even he would have been dumbfounded to know what we know now about the incredible vastness of the universe in which our tiny globe moves and has its being. Niebuhr's statement, then, appears to be wholly justified — man is put summarily and uncomfortably in his place!

The insignificance of man, which emerges from modern scientific studies, clashes sharply with and ridicules the popular understanding of the Christian view of man. Doesn't the Bible say that God created the world in six days? Doesn't it assert that God created Adam and Eve, our forefathers, and that Eve was made of Adam's rib? Doesn't it, furthermore, trace all of man's evil back to that unfortunate picnic in the Garden? 'An apple one day brought the devil to stay,' mocks John Weightman.[2]

Christians may protest that this picture is a travesty of the Biblical teaching. The fact remains, however, that the contrast between the coherent plausibility of the modern view which makes God unnecessary for a doctrine of man, and the apparent mythology of the Jewish-Christian account of man's origin, is so great that argument is unnecessary. The battle for the minds of men has been won in the classroom.

But even within the Christian Church there are mature and intelligent people whose scientific training and professional knowledge of the nature of man have never been systematically related to the Christian faith. One is puzzled why this is so. Is it because of some feeling that the Church would resist an attempt to bring Christian teaching into line with scientific views? Or could the real reason be that many lay Christians are afraid that the Christian view of man will not bear the weight of the questions they would bring?

But those who follow a man who claimed to be 'the way, *the truth* and the life' have nothing to fear from the truth, neither will they wish to suppress enquiry or research. Authentic Christianity claims, on the contrary, that its view of man is coherent, and relevant, and worthy of the serious attention of modern man.

The Interpretation of Genesis 1-3

Although the Bible does not provide a definitive dogmatic answer to the question 'What is man?' which it asks occasionally (Ps. 8:4; 144:7), it is quite apparent that the Genesis account of man's origin is of the utmost significance for Christian belief. Although Genesis 1-3 is referred to rarely in the rest of the Bible, it cannot be removed from the Christian view of man, because it is the backcloth against which the entire Christian story is set.

But with this account of man's origin we encounter the problem of interpretation. Is it an historical account, couched in the language and thought terms of a primitive and scientifically naïve culture? A myth? A fairy story of no more relevance than the *Arabian Nights*, although rather less interesting?

There are two factors we must carefully isolate: the purpose of the Genesis account and the literary genre (style) in which it is expressed. The purpose is *not* to give a scientific account of the creation of the world and the rise of mankind. This needs to be emphasised because some non-Christian thinkers still assume that this is the point of the story! It is not. Genesis 1 is not explaining *how* the world began, but *who* began it. It is the subject and object of creation that is the concern of the writer — God and the created order — and not the mechanics of the process. The terse statements that begin, 'and God said, let there be...' tell in simple words that all things are the work of God. Genesis 1 is expressing in a more dramatic form the statement of Psalm 19 that 'the heavens are telling the glory of God and the firmament proclaims his handiwork'. It is important to keep before us, therefore, the fact that Genesis 1-3 is concerned primarily with theology and not science or history.

Following the straightforward narrative of the creation, the story of man is expressed in Chapter 2 in a simple story which embodies profound symbolism. To treat this particular passage as a historical document is to make nonsense of its meaning. The garden, the woman made from the rib, the serpent, the trees, the apple, God walking in the garden, and the flaming sword are all anthropomorphic expressions of man's relationship to God. It is highly doubtful that the writer intended these forms to be taken literally. To take but one of these elements, can we really support the view that the writer meant his readers to think of God taking a walk in a real garden? It would be entirely contrary to the steady emphasis throughout the Old Testament upon the transcendance of God and his difference from man. The nature of the Genesis account, therefore, implies that we are dealing with material that is highly parabolic in character, in which theological meaning must be very carefully distinguished from the setting. In case this interpretation should be misconstrued as the casuistry of a Christian covering his tracks, we should remember that long before the modern era a symbolic interpretation was common to both Hebrew as well as Christian thinkers.[3] We need to realise that the cosmology, zoology, biology and ethnology of the Bible are not binding in any form. Biblical ideas and knowledge provide the alphabet in which God works and writes, but they need constant retranslation into modern terms. John Calvin was wrong to challenge Copernicus's discovery that the earth went round the sun by quoting Psalm 93 that 'The world is established and it shall never be moved'. The truth of that saying is not harmed by the removal of the implicit cosmology of the Psalmist. To take another example, we have known for a long time that the 'heart' is not the centre of the emotions or the seat of intellectual life, but that does not affect in the slightest the *meaning* of Jeremiah's statement that 'the heart is desperately wicked and who shall know it?' Perhaps the prophet did believe the heart was the mainspring of man's mental activity, but the validity of what he wrote is not at all impugned.

Evolution and the Bible

In November 1859 Charles Darwin published his famous book *On the Origin of Species* and so sparked off a terrific explosion in religious and scientific circles. His research, which suggested that nature had painfully and slowly evolved by means of natural selection, challenged the religious basis of human society. The idea that there is in nature a constant struggle for existence in which the weakest go to the wall, posed searching questions concerning the providence of God and his work in the world. Men were appalled by the implications; the extent of suffering seemed beyond comprehension and utterly pointless. Lord Tennyson gave graphic expression to the shock in these well known words:

> Are God and nature then at strife
> That nature lends such evil dreams?
> So careful of the type she seems
> So careless of the single life.
> That I considering everywhere
> Her secret meaning in her deeds,

> And finding that of fifty seeds
> She often brings but one to bear,
> I falter where I firmly trod...[4]

Lord Tennyson faltered, and the Church was aghast. It seemed to many Christians that the very foundation of faith had been shattered by Darwinism. Sadly, but perhaps inevitably, the Church began a fierce counter-attack against the evolutionary hypothesis. It was sad because Christians assumed automatically that the new ideas were wrong, atheistic, and contrary to belief; it was inevitable, because of the claims and counter-claims that were being made in the name of science and religion. The focal point of the controversy came into the famous debate between Thomas Huxley and Bishop Wilberforce in the summer of 1860. Wilberforce, talented and able as he was, was routed by the brilliant case prepared by Darwin and presented by Huxley. 'Was it through your grandfather or your grandmother that you claim descent from the monkeys?' taunted the Bishop. Huxley's reply really amounted to the retort that he would prefer to have a monkey for an ancestor than a Bishop! Little could come out of exchanges like that, and the humiliation of Wilberforce was the humiliation of the Church. Even today when people talk about the 'conflict' between religion and science they really have the nineteenth century controversy over evolution in mind.

In point of fact that historic confrontation between the two great leaders was both unfortunate and unnecessary. The atmosphere was so emotionally charged that little but harm could come out of it. For many Christians thereafter evolution was a dirty word. Even in the famous University Church of St. Mary the Virgin, Oxford, a well-known preacher thundered 'leave my ancestors in Paradise and I will leave yours in the zoological gardens'. Perhaps it wasn't so surprising that many evolutionists dismissed religion as nothing but an obstacle to the progress of knowledge. To be sure there was a small nucleus of distinguished people on both sides who urged restraint. Some theologians, led by F. J. A. Hort at Cambridge, hailed the theory as a great contribution to the knowledge of mankind. And moderate biologists attempted to temper the wild scientific claims made by followers and popularisers of Darwin and his equally important contemporary, Alfred Wallace. Actually, the debate was never between science and the Bible, but between different interpretations of science; the Bible was thought to support one and the evolutionary theory another.

In many ways the Biblical story of Creation is far removed from the fierce controversy outlined. It is only when the Biblical account is treated as being an explicit opponent to modern theories that it is brought into a head-on collision. Indeed, the reverse may be said; although we have no intention of producing a 'concordant' treatment between science and the Bible, it is extraordinary how the Biblical narrative anticipates an evolutionary pattern. The progress of creation developing from 'light', then on to firmament, water, earth, vegetation, creatures in the sea, birds, creatures on land, and man as the final creation, has a fairly modern 'feel' about it. The Bible, in fact, contrasts sharply with many other ancient cosmologies that place men at the beginning of the series of created beings. Furthermore, the modern idea of creation as an ever continuous and developing phenomenon finds strong confirmation in Christian theology. Although Genesis appears to view creation as a completed act, as it is in one sense, it is obvious that God's constant and loving interest in his creative work reveals him as one who continually 'makes all things new'. He governs and sustains his creation. He is not an 'absentee' God whose work is over, but one who is still at work. Jesus's words to the Jews who objected to his healing on the Sabbath that 'My father works hitherto and I work' (John 5:17) point to the ever present activity of God. But we must be careful of attempts to fit the Bible into a scientific framework, however attractive appear to be the similarities, because the Bible gives us no encouragement to do so and fresh scientific discoveries will only alter the picture. The Bible is content to say *God created* and makes no attempt to prove it. It is taken as self-evident that the proof is all around us.

Christian faith, in short, has nothing to fear from a theory of evolution which accepts the notion of God's activity within it. So Mgr. de Hulst puts it; 'Yes, with God at the beginning of existence, God at the end of the process, God by the side of the columns to uphold it and direct its movement, evolution is admissible'.[5] It was, in fact, the impersonal, mechanistic, purposeless features of Darwinism that many people, not only Christians, could not accept because it contradicted their own experience of life. Even though Darwin concluded his magnum opus with the belief that in creation 'there is a grandeur in this view of life, with its several powers, having been originally breathed by the Creator into a few forms or one', the force of his work seemed to be a formidable case for a cruel and meaningless universe. Since Darwin's time, however, many thinkers have supported the view that we should allow for a purposive element within natural selection itself. As is well known, Teilhard de Chardin believed consciousness to be the key to evolution. He contended that far from being blind and opportunist, progress is meaningful because there is a conscious element in matter which reaches its highest form of development in the emergence of consciousness in man.[6] Sir Julian Huxley, while he cannot share Teilhard's Christian vision, largely identified himself with the approach. He applauded Teilhard's threefold synthesis of matter with mind, past with future, and variety with unity. He also agreed that the whole of reality should be seen not as a static mechanism, but as a process.[7] True, Teilhard's thesis has received opposition, as any serious and important work does, but the significance of it lies in the emphasis it gives to the whole of the natural order and to the possibility of approaching it from a theistic point of view. In his opinion, there is enough evidence that evolution is not a purposeless, blind, merry-go-round, but a purposeful process with a 'precise orientation' and a 'privileged axis'. Sir Alistair Hardy, though he disapproves of Teilhard's poetic imagination in expressing a scientific account, also refuses to accept that materialism is central to evolution. The whole of creation, in his view, is a living stream in which consciousness is an integral element 'and in which religion is a fundamental feature of man's make-up'.[8]

The uniqueness of man

But where the Christian may be most disturbed by the

challenge of the evolutionary theory is, perhaps, in the popular idea that it has exploded all those long-cherished ideas and Biblically rooted illusions about man's separateness from, and superiority over, 'brute creation'. There is no need, it is said, to appeal to any hypothesis outside nature to interpret his existence. Although only a newcomer on the stage of world history, he is descended from the family of man (hominidae) in which many noble, yet savage, forbears have acted out their brief career. Through fossil remains we may trace our ancestors through Cro-Magnon man, Neanderthal man, the Pithecanthropus group of Java, the Sinanthropus species of China and perhaps back over two million years to the much disputed remains of Australopithecus africanus, the Southern ape-man. So much, it seems, for the mystique of man.

Modern man's place in the natural order may be seen vividly in terms of a time scale telescoped into twelve calendar months. Let us suppose that the world had its origin on January 1st. Life then appears on July 22nd, mammals arrive on December 20th and hominoids only on December 28th. And at eleven thirty p.m. on December 31st modern man makes his late entry!

There are two errors that one can make when assessing the importance of man. The first is to assert that he is merely an animal and must be treated accordingly, and the second is to place man outside the natural order altogether. We can dismiss the last idea at once, for it is contradicted by both natural sciences and the Bible. But the view that man is *nothing but* an animal is emphasised by some thinkers. Long ago Max Scheler contended that 'between an intelligent monkey and an Edison, merely a technical intelligence, only a difference of degree exists'.[9] More recently, Henry Miller, Vice-Chancellor of Newcastle University, in a radio broadcast, defined man as 'an enormously intelligent and intellectually agile animal'.[10] It is obvious that a quantitative difference exists between man and animals, but may we talk of a qualitative difference? Traditional definitions have tried to encapsulate the distinctiveness of man by picking out distinctive characteristics. So for example, he is defined as 'homo faber', tool-maker; 'homo ludens', the player; 'homo religiosus', a religious creature; 'homo sapiens', an intelligent creature. But because such definitions are too general, we must cite those characteristics which seem to be distinctly human activities. Man, it is usually said, stands out because of:

1   The development of language
2   His inventiveness and creative skill
3   Religious longings and awareness of death as a threat to fulfilment as a person
4   The creation of culture
5   Symbolical and conceptual thought
6   The production of literature
7   The awareness of moral laws which transcend him.

It is often argued that many of the above distinctions are found in animals, although at a much lower level. Language is known in other creatures, for example. This is true, but a world of difference exists between the simple signals of birds and animals and the infinitely versatile speech of humans.[11] Man's speech can probe past and future as well as present; and new ideas, new words, are constantly being invented. Linked to human speech is man's great power of rationality and criticism. He can 'abstract', that is, take out from the various forms of expression the crucial content; he can 'conceptualise', that is, understand and express complex ideas often with a highly symbolical and elaborate content. Perhaps a method of teaching the use of language to young chimpanzees will one day be developed. But such an achievement must not be interpreted as narrowing significantly the gap between the two species, because it would still be man's language which would form the basis of communication. Such a feat could only enhance the ability of man himself.

The presence of religion throughout man's history should also be considered. Wherever we look into man's past we find him conscious of a realm beyond himself. Of course, some might object: just because primitive people share the taste for religion this doesn't mean to say it is true. After all, religion may be practised for the wrong reasons — fear, or superstition. Agreed, but all the same it speaks of a universal human concern with the things beyond this life. To dismiss this as something that belongs to man's primitive childhood is like sawing off the branch upon which we sit. As E. L. Mascall once remarked, 'It indicates how abnormal in human history secularism is.'

Even though many of man's capacities are developments of qualities already present in higher animals, in practically every area of life the gulf between man and other creatures is vast and deep. We have to ask then, when do differences of degree become to all intents and purposes a difference of kind? The degree of difference we are dealing with can be compared with the change from a caterpillar to a butterfly, or perhaps the interaction of hydrogen with oxygen to produce water. In both cases, as in man, no absolute discontinuity is evident, but real differences in kind have emerged from real differences in degree. Perhaps the word 'emergence', in fact, is the key to our understanding of the difference between man and other beings. If, for example, we analyse man in terms of his parts — speech, physical organism, social organisation and so on — there only appear differences of degree. But entities are never fully comprehended in terms of their constituent parts. Rather, in some qualitative sense the whole is 'more' than the sum of its parts. A new 'kind' of creature emerges.[12]

The enormous gap between man and other created beings leads us to question the implied reductionism of such popular writers as Konrad Lorenz, Desmond Morris and Robert Ardrey.[13] Their common approach, based on the assumption of man's identity with the animal world, is that because man is an animal, studies of the behaviour of animals and their inter-relationship with the environment throw light upon human behaviour and give important clues for the progress of humanity. Thus, after comparing humanity with the higher primates, Morris comments on human civilisation that 'we are all naked apes beneath the wide variety of our adopted costumes'.[14] In a later work *The Human Zoo*, he interprets human society in the light of observations upon animals in captivity, and makes many deductions about the nature and future well-being of civilisation on the basis of these comparisons. There is much that is helpful, interesting and delightfully

entertaining in Morris's books, but there are some astonishing
logical and anthropological blunders as well. To take but one:
he says of human society that 'bearing in mind our monkey
ancestry, the social organisation of surviving monkey species
can provide us with some revealing clues'.[15] It is remarkable
that such an able zoologist as Morris has forgotten (or
ignored) the fact that man is not descended from one of the
anthropoid species of ape still existent. The current evolutionary view assumes that ape and man constitute two branches
of the process. There is no compelling reason why the
constitution of monkey society should provide a better mirror
for mankind to hold up to itself than that of, say, the hyena.
Robert Ardrey agrees, but falls into the opposite error — he
fails to discriminate between the bewildering variety of
species, with the result that everything in animal behaviour is
grist to his mill! Certainly, examination of the effects of
environment upon animals shows some similarities to human
behaviour and can help forward our understanding of the
human condition. For example, experiments with rats under
crowded conditions have been of some help in showing us the
danger of pressure in high-density areas of inner-city housing.
So we talk of rat-race, but very few people will try to overdo
the relationship between rats and humanity! The 'compara-
tive method', of course, is a very useful tool for the zoologist
and anthropologist but it must be used with the greatest
caution. Wild claims can only bring discredit upon those who
make them. If projections of animal behaviour are applied to
human society some explanation concerning the limitations
of the study should accompany them.

   The *nothing but* interpretation, in stressing an integral link
between animal and human behaviour, is of great significance to the debate about man as a moral being. Indeed, if
man is 'nothing but an animal', moral blame cannot be laid
at his door for living up (or down) to his nature. To be sure,
he can be chided for not acting according to his greater
intelligence but he need not feel guilty about emotions and
drives which belong to the residual animality at the heart of
his nature. So, for example, Ardrey in exploring man's
aggression comes to the conclusion that if it belongs to man's
essential nature, 'man is an innate killer'.[16] This means, in

fact, that it becomes exceedingly difficult to blame him for
aggression which is as normal for him as having apple pie for
lunch.

Reductionism of this kind, with its basic principle of
applied zoology, does not do justice to the concept of man. It
may also be that such an approach represents a distortion of
the animal world because of the eagerness to trace similarities
with mankind. But the fact remains that such attempts do
not take into sufficient account the humanity of man. Indeed,
it is ironic that secular man is always prone to protect his
humanity in the face of oppression and ill-treatment. In such
circumstances he is not so keen to be treated as animal or a
thing without value. He expects to be treated as a person with
inalienable rights.

What about Adam?

We observed earlier that while modern man is a compara-
tive newcomer on earth his origins are lost in the mists of
antiquity. Even though it is generally acknowledged that
man's evolutionary links go right back into the mainstream of
animal life, no clear evidence of the step from animal life to
humanity has yet come to light. There are still great gaps in
the fossil record and, even after many amazing discoveries of
pre-historic human remains, we are still left with the mystery
of man's origin. Of course, palaeontologists remind us that
the chances of finding the fossilised remains of the first of any
species are extremely slight. When, as the result of mutation,
a new species appears, its numbers are very small. Chance
dictates whether they will fossilise in the first place, and the
odds that they will be dug up much later are very long
indeed. The arrogant, self-assured expectation of early evolutionists that before long man's origins would be tabulated
and catalogued minutely, has been displaced by the more
humble and tentative approach of modern scientists. 'The key
to the secret door through which we came into the world is
still unknown,' admits the anthropologist Loren Eiseley, and
he appeals for a deeper sense of wonder at the universe in
which mankind is set.[17]

This tantalisingly incomplete story of man encourages some

people to raise from time to time the question of Adam, attempting to fit him into this complex, uncertain and mysterious history. But such a temptation should and must be resisted for two reasons. First of all, concordant theories are based, as we observed earlier, on a misunderstanding of the Genesis account. The story in Genesis expresses man as a being made by God and for God. The picturesque and symbolic nature of the passage indicates that we risk much and lose much if we seek to historicise it. If some still want to insist, it is possible that the narrative is describing the experience of the first man after he has crossed the threshold from 'ape-man' into full manhood, by personally receiving the 'inbreathing' of God, but we must remind them that this cannot be proved and furthermore would appear to be far removed from the intention of the writer. We must beware of a type of a 'God of the gaps' theology which tries to substantiate Christian belief by attempting to fit it into gaps in the scientific record. Of course, the current hypothesis of the monophylitic origin of mankind, that humanity originated from a single evolving population and later diversified into races, may lend support to the Biblical idea of man, but the Christian must beware of the temptation to jump on the latest bandwagon. To keep up with the scientific 'Joneses' is no way to gain credibility or respect. It is one thing to show that Christianity is credible to modern people — it is quite another to prop it up with pseudo-scientific assumptions.

Secondly, concordant theories appear to assume defensively that science is an obstacle to faith and revelation. Surely God is the author of the natural 'laws' discovered by science, just as he is of the revelation in the Biblical record? Ultimately there cannot be a real contradiction between the two. Occasionally, the Christian has to fight 'scientism', which is the materialistic and one-dimensional view which makes science the only touchstone and arbiter of truth. But such an attitude is quite rare in modern scientific circles.

So we must say a firm 'no' to two dangers: on the one hand, the danger of assuming that the Genesis story is merely a historical and factual account of man's origin, and on the other, the temptation of making science or a branch within it definitive for truth. But modern study of the Bible together

with our growing knowledge of man's complex origins have
helped us see that the Genesis account must be interpreted,
not as a cosmological and anthropological record, but as a
Word from the Lord reminding man in every generation of
his nature and God-given humanity. The validation of such
a statement is found not in some proof from the past — such
as Adam's birth certificate — but in the way it speaks to men
in their situation and describes their true condition.

Man — nature's riddle?

Perhaps the most significant contribution of modern anthropology is that it has given back to man his capacity to
wonder and to be in awe, not only at his similarity to other
creatures, but also at his difference from them. Whereas early
studies seemed intent on replacing one set of dogmas with
another, modern research with less dogmatism and with
greater knowledge has shown us what a puzzle mankind
really is. Secular man may denigrate the 'wasteful and
clumsy mechanism of natural selection' but we cannot fail to
be amazed at the capacity of such a 'process' to produce
beings with such moral, spiritual and intellectual responses.
Man may be a product of nature, but one who participates
actively in the process, to such an extent that, for good or ill,
he can also alter it. 'In mankind evolution has become
conscious of itself,' comments Julian Huxley.[18] Yet the
question why out of two million species of organisms this can
only be said of man is a mystery. We may grant that the
differences between man and animals are quantitative, yet so
many are they and so large is the gap that they become to all
intents and purposes qualitative. Man stands out from other
animals and outstrips his self-explanations.

The Christian replies, however, that man will always
remain a riddle if the questions and answers are put within a
naturalist framework. Man, he will continue, becomes explic-
able only when God is brought into the picture. Indeed, the
early chapters of Genesis have the correct balance in three
clear ideas they express. Firstly, that man is a natural
creature, subject to earth. Secondly, that man is radically
different from other creatures, not on the basis of superior

gifts, but because of a direct and unique relationship between man and God. Thirdly, that into man alone has God 'breathed'; that is to say, only man among creatures is spiritual, because the life of God indwells him. In short, man without God is a denial of true humanity, and we are back with riddles again.

NOTES

1 R. Niebuhr, *The Nature and Destiny of Man* (Nisbet, 1941), I, p. 3.
2 J. Weightman, *The Concept of the Avant-garde* (Alcove Press, 1973), p. 69.
3 Within Judaism Philo and his followers advanced such ideas. Christian thinkers in the early Church include Clement of Alexandria, Origen and Ambrose.
4 *In Memoriam*, A.H.H.LV.
5 Quoted by Henri Rondet, S. J., in *Original Sin* (Ecclesia Press, 1972).
6 *The Phenomenon of Man* (Collins, 1959).
7 Foreword to *The Phenomenon of Man.*
8 *The Living Stream* (Collins, 1965), p. 295. See also T. Dobzhansky, *The Biology of Ultimate Concern* (Fontana, 1971).
9 *Die Stellung des Menschen in Kosmos,* p. 46.
10 See *The Listener*, July 1st, 1971.
11 See R. Ascher, 'The Human Revolution', *Current Anthropology* 5, pp. 135-168, 1964.
12 Read M. Polanyi, *The Tacit Dimension*, 1967; also P. Davies, *The Month*, March 1972, for an excellent discussion of this problem.
13 K. Lorenz, *King Solomon's Ring* (Methuen, 1952). D. Morris, *The Naked Ape* (Cape, 1967). R. Ardrey, *African Genesis* (Collins, 1961).
14 *The Naked Ape*, p. 146.
15 *The Human Zoo* (Cape, 1969), p. 21.
16 *African Genesis*, p. 182.
17 *The Unexpected Universe* (Penguin, 1973).
18 Julian Huxley, *Essays of a Humanist* (Penguin, 1966), p. 72ff.

CHAPTER 2

Man as God's Creature

G. K. CHESTERTON once wrote, 'We have all read in scientific books, and indeed in all romance, about the man who has forgotten his name. The man walks about the streets and can see and appreciate everything; only he cannot remember who he is. Well, everyman is that man in the story.'[1] From a Christian point of view, the problem of man's identity is bound up with his relationship to God. Man is not sure who he is because he has lost contact with the one who gives him identity and meaning. So the Christian faith speaks to the secular world: 'You reject God and claim to have no need of him in order to run your lives, and yet you value man and seek to find a true definition of him. Until God is brought back into the picture your whole idea of man is bound to be faulty and incomplete.'

It is, in fact, with God that the Christian doctrine of man begins; God the transcendent and self-sufficient One who calls all things into being. The emphasis upon the distinction between God and nature, between God and everything else, starts in the creation narratives and continues throughout the Bible. God is 'wholly other' declared the theologian Rudolph Otto, meaning by this that he does not need anything or anyone to explain him. Those unfamiliar with the Bible are often astonished when they find out how exalted and transcendent is the Old Testament concept of God, when perhaps they were assuming and expecting a rather pedestrian and terrestrial view of the deity. On the contrary, the

Bible stresses that God is almighty, the creator and sustainer of all things, utterly unlike idols made in man's image.

Before this awe-inspiring concept of God, man is put very firmly in his place. He stands within the natural order and according to the Bible there is no basic difference in the physical makeup of animals and man. He also is flesh (Heb. *basar*), and made of the 'dust of the ground' (Gen. 2:7). No humanist could speak more definitely of man's lowly origins. Man — the scriptures tell us — is a created being, finite and natural. Like other creatures he is born, procreates, eats, excretes, suffers and dies. The very idea of 'dust' describes man's creaturely status. The psalm which declares that 'when you take away their breath they die and return to their dust' (Ps. 104:29) is speaking of all creation, man included.

Nevertheless, while the Bible plainly puts man within the created order it provides some clues, in the terms it uses to describe man's nature, to suggest that humanity transcends material existence. Although many words are used by the Bible to describe man's psychology and physical nature, in the description of man as *soul*, *spirit*, and *image* we have profound insights into man's relationship to God.

The first clue comes from the description of man as *soul*, which approximates to two Biblical words — the Old Testament *nephesh*, and the New Testament term, *psyche*. The pitfall for the unwary is to assume that man *has* a soul, as if he has an independent element within him. This idea is foreign not only to the Old Testament but to the Bible as a whole. *Nephesh* is derived from a word meaning 'throat' or 'gullet', and by extension came to mean that 'which proceeds from the throat'. We might say it is the 'breath of life' or 'life' itself. When a man's breath goes, he goes! *Nephesh* equals life. So Elijah complains to God 'they seek my *nephesh* to take it away' (I Kings 19:14). *Nephesh* is also closely associated with 'blood'. This connection is easy to understand; if a man's blood is shed his life ebbs away, so the Hebrew naturally thought that the essence of life lay in the blood. The Old Testament could also think in terms of degrees of life and death. So the *nephesh* can be emptied (Isa. 53:12) or it may be full. This may seem a strange idea to modern people who think in terms of creatures either being alive or dead. But we

must remember that in ordinary conversation we also talk
about feeling 'half dead' or 'full of life' or, we might say of
someone, 'there's plenty of life in the old boy yet!' The
Hebrews were not alone in being imprecise.

The New Testament word *psyche* also represents life. 'Take
no thought for your *psyche*,' urged Jesus, giving his teaching
about facing anxiety, 'what you shall eat or what you shall
drink or what you shall put on. Is not life more than food and
the body more than clothing?' (Matt. 6:25). But *psyche* could
also be used to stand for 'people' as in the description of
Paul's shipwreck in Acts 27:37 where, we are told, '276
psychai' were saved.

The terms *nephesh* and *psyche*, however, cannot be limited to
a description of man as a living and natural being. *Nephesh* is
used very frequently in the Bible to describe man's desire for
God; it expresses the totality of human nature caught up in
love and wonder. 'Bless the Lord, O my *nephesh*, and all that
is within me bless his holy name' cries the psalmist in
exultation (Ps. 103:1). If we thought only in terms of its literal
translation we would have to translate this, 'bless the Lord, O
my throat'! It is obvious that the writer is stressing the totality
of life and, at the heart of it, man as a being capable of
spiritual responses to God. The New Testament also uses the
word *psyche* in the same way. Jesus's warning that 'whoever
will save his *psyche* shall lose it, and whoever shall lose it for
my sake and the gospel's shall gain it' (Matt. 16:25) shows the
continuity between the earthly and heavenly life of man.
Man does not possess a *psyche*, as if it were a suitcase or an
umbrella, but he *is* a *psyche*. This life comes from God and is
for God. The rich fool of Luke 12:19 was foolish not because
he was rich, but because his life ignored the spiritual
dimension; therefore his *psyche* was required of him.

The second clue we find in the Bible is in the application of
the term 'spirit' to man. This in some ways is surprising in
view of the transcendence of God because the Hebrew word
ruach meaning wind, is mainly used in the Old Testament of
God's nature and his activity in the world. In the earliest part
of the Bible, for example, *ruach* was not considered to be a
normal constituent of man's nature, and when applied to
human beings described a temporary invasion of man's

personality for specific purposes. Mighty men of God, like Samson, did their mighty works when the Spirit (*ruach*) of God came upon them (Judges 14:6; 1 Sam. 11:6). In later writings *ruach* gradually began to be treated as part of man's personality, describing those functions of a higher kind connected with understanding and ethical intentions. Indeed in many ways *ruach* becomes virtually synonymous with *nephesh* and *leb* (heart) which was considered to be the intellectual and volitional centre of man. Ezekiel uses 'spirit' and 'heart' together when he prophesies the indwelling of a new spirit as well as a new heart (Ezek. 11:19; 18:3; 36:26). So what is the particular significance of *ruach* when used of man? The importance of the term lies in its origin. Contrary to *nephesh*, the *ruach* is something that is particularly associated with God. When used of man it links him uniquely, specially, to God the Spirit, creator and sustainer of all.

The same may be said of the New Testament word for Spirit (*pneuma*). Like the term *ruach* the Greek equivalent is used mainly of the Spirit of God and it is from this centre that it gets its significance. But we find one important advance upon the Old Testament is that the term, when used of man, is generally applied to Christians, who alone are indwelt by the Spirit of God. This usage is particularly true of Paul. So much so that H. W. Robinson claims that Paul's doctrine of the Spirit is 'his most important and characteristic contribution to Christian anthropology'.[2] According to Paul, the Spirit is given to all those who know 'Jesus as Lord' (1 Cor. 12:3), and now through the Spirit they have fellowship with God and access into heavenly realities (1 Cor. 2: 10-16).

This description of man as *soul* and man as *spirit* must not, of course, be misconstrued as implying that man is composed of different and self-contained compartments. It is clear that the Biblical authors wrote and spoke on the firm assumption of man's psychosomatic unity. Yet, in the use of such terms we see the emergence of an understanding of man as a being made for God and dissatisfied apart from him. He is a creature certainly, but he is God's creature who gropes for relationship with God and fulfilment in him.

MAN AS GOD'S IMAGE

Important as are the terms 'soul' and 'spirit' the clearest clue for the spiritual nature of man is found in the breathtaking notion that man is made in God's *image*. This, according to Genesis, is the difference between man and other creatures. In the command 'Let us make man in our image, after our likeness' (Gen. 1:26), we have described the beginning of a new creative act and a wholly different relationship between creator and creature. Man alone is made in God's image.

But what does it mean and what is its significance? Perhaps no other Biblical text has had as much attention as this one, and still great differences of interpretation exist concerning its precise meaning. Some, for example have seen in the idea a suggestion of a physical likeness. This finds some support in Genesis 5:1 where it is said of Adam that he had become 'father of a son in his own *likeness*, after his *image*, and named him Seth'. In Babylonian myths, we note, man is made in the physical likeness of the deity. But an idea of a physical representation is far too limiting when we take into account the emphasis in Genesis 1, and elsewhere, upon the transcendence of God. The stress of the passage is not upon some physical identity, but rather that man is a being who belongs by nature not to the earth, but transcends it because he belongs to God.

Another mistaken interpretation is that 'image' and 'likeness' refer to two different elements within man's nature. In the second century, Irenaeus distinguished between the two words to account for the fallen nature of man. He argued that man's likeness (*demuth*) referred to man's original righteousness which was lost at the Fall, while the image (*zelem*) — man as a rational and free being — continues to exist in fallen man. At first sight this seems a plausible view, because if man fell he must have lost something of great importance. Irenaeus' idea prevailed until the Reformation when Luther pointed out that in this phrase we have but a common Hebrew parallelism: the second term merely repeating, or possibly defining more closely the image, to show that a spiritual meaning is intended.

When we try, however, to discover what is the precise

content of the phrase 'made in our image' we are handicapped by the fact that nowhere in the Bible do we find a definition of this puzzling idea. It seems clear, then, that the context of Genesis 1:26 is of the greatest importance in our quest for its meaning. In this passage we meet three significant elements which not only shed light on the meaning of the 'image' idea but which also challenge modern concepts of human nature. Indeed, we find that because man is made in God's image, certain responsibilities and obligations follow from this status. These duties cannot be separated from the 'image' idea. It is precisely *because* he is made in God's image that those responsibilities are conferred upon him. As such we should expect them to shed considerable light upon the meaning of the image. Neither should we be surprised if they challenge modern concepts of human nature and man's relationship to his environment.

(a) Man is a co-worker with God

Man created in God's likeness is called to have dominion over the rest of the created order. 'Be fruitful and multiply and fill the earth and subdue it, and have dominion over the fish of the sea and over the birds of the air and over every living thing that moves over the earth' (Gen. 1:28). Here we find an indication that the creativity of God does not cease with the physical creation of the world. God continues his work through the continuing activity of mankind to whom is delegated the task of giving it order, structure and beauty. This idea meets head-on the opinion expressed by D. H. Lawrence in *Women in Love*, that 'there would be no absolute loss if every human being perished tomorrow...man is the mistake of creation'. On the contrary, according to the Bible, man is not a mistake but the fulfilment of creation. Genesis explicitly states that the world without man is incomplete and unfinished. Creation was awaiting man to 'till the ground and to keep it' (2:5). It is not too much to say that man is the crowning achievement of God's creative work. Although divine satisfaction could be expressed after each stage of creation (vv. 12, 18, 21, 24) only after the climax of man's creation was it possible to say 'God saw everything that he had made, and behold it was very good' (v. 31). In creating man God completes his activity and in obedience to God man continues God's creativity.

This theocentric approach to the world challenges two common tendencies in the modern world. This first, common to Eastern religions, is to blur the distinction between God, man and nature, leading to a glorification of nature, so that all is divinised. The second temptation, common in the western world, is to divide man from nature. This, a side effect of industrialisation, has led to an anthropocentric attitude towards nature, so that it becomes something to exploit or use for man's comfort. It is difficult for modern industrial man to deny that his education and way of life tend towards an anti-nature bias in his attitude to his environment.

However, John Passmore, the philosopher, argues to the contrary that Christianity must take a major share of the blame in the denigration of nature. He insists that Christianity's anthropocentric attitude to the world has 'led to an arrogant attitude to life'. For him, the emphasis upon the Incarnation — God taking human form — is undeniable proof that the Christian faith has a faulty and distorted doctrine of creation.[3] There is, we must concede, some ground to such criticisms; Christian teaching has sometimes encouraged mankind to consider itself far superior to everything else and free to treat nature as it likes. But this failure is not due to a faulty theology of nature but to two different reasons. The first is an over-spiritualising of salvation so that all that matters is the soul; the second and most crucial reason is the failure of the Church to take seriously the Old Testament teaching concerning nature. When this is done Passmore's criticisms are silenced most effectively because the Old Testament demonstrates God's concern for the whole of his creation. 'He owns every beast in the forest and the cattle upon a thousand hills' (Ps. 50:10) and he cares for them all (Gen. 8:17, 9:10; Job 38:26-7; Ps. 104:10-11). Indeed, Passmore's attack on the theological basis of nature also fails to take into account Jesus' own attitude towards nature which comes out vividly in his teaching; a love of the created world and a belief in a Providence which is not careless of the birds of the air (Matt. 6:25ff, 10:29).

The role of man as God's co-worker, we suggest, is a very significant element in the ideas surrounding the term 'image'. To use David Jenkins' phrase, man 'stands out' from the created order not as a tyrant or despot over nature, but in his moral and intellectual capabilities as governor of God's world.[4] This role he must exercise wisely, lovingly, and unselfishly, recognising that he has to give account to God.

(b) Man as a responsible being

Although a co-worker with God, man is under God's authority and answerable to him. Man is given dominion and told to subdue the earth but he is not given permission to exploit it or use it selfishly. 'All things' are indeed 'put under his feet' as Psalm 8 declares; 'all sheep and oxen and also the beasts of the field' (v. 7) are under man's dominion, but a recognition of a symbiosis between all living things is tacitly assumed in the Old Testament. In the ancient laws of Israel one of man's duties was to respect life and submit himself to the order of creation (Exod. 23:19; Deut. 22.9ff). Here we find the insight that man disturbs the delicate harmony of nature at his own peril, and when this happens he travesties his position as steward of God's world. If in our own day we face the bleak prospect of a bankrupt and exhausted world, much of the blame must be placed at the feet of modern man for failing to face up to the responsibility of being God's agent in the world. In the Bible this responsibility is worked out in three main ways; to man as creature, to man as a moral being, and to man as worshipper.

(i) *Man as creature.* However unique man is in creation and however great are his achievements, he must remember his origin — he is but dust before God. Ironically, while modern man claims to be aware of his own finite and insignificant character he contradicts it by usurping God's place as head of all. Denying the relevance and existence of God he claims for himself 'squatter's rights'. Edmund Leach represents this position when he opened the Reith Lecture of 1967 with these words: 'Men have become like gods. Isn't it about time that we understood our divinity? Science offers us total mastery over our environment and over our destiny, yet instead of rejoicing we feel deeply afraid.'[5] The arrogance and self-assurance of the anthropocentric view contrasts sharply with Psalm 8 which paints a more realistic picture. To start with, the greatness of God is acknowledged; 'O Lord, Our Lord, how majestic is thy name in all the earth;' and the psalmist looks at God's creation, 'the heavens, the work of thy fingers, the moon and the stars which thou hast established'. It is as if the writer had a modern view of the vastness of the solar system and in the face of this was aware of the distance between Almighty God and mankind. He marvels, 'What is man that thou art mindful of him and the son of man that thou dost care for him?' The realism of the psalmist concerning man's finiteness and insufficiency is very apparent, and this refrain is picked up in many other passages of the Old Testament. Psalm 103, for example, comments on man's nature, 'as for man his days are like grass; he flourishes like a flower of the field, for the wind passes over it and it is gone and the place knows it no more' (15-16). But this is no credo for nihilism and despair, because it is recognised that man's finiteness binds him in creaturely dependence to his creator. Thus the psalmist returns to the theme of the eternal mercy of God: 'but the steadfast love of the Lord is from everlasting to everlasting upon those who fear him' (v. 17). R. Niebuhr aptly remarks: 'the fragmentary character of human life is not regarded as evil in Biblical faith because it is seen from the perspective of a centre of life in which each fragment is related to the plan of the whole, to the will of God'.[6]

A rediscovery of the Biblical doctrine of man as a creature is necessary if there is to be any real change of heart in man's relationship to the created world. The 'technological' model of man as above nature must be replaced by the biological and Biblical truth of man as in nature. We must take seriously the biological reality of the human situation and understand that man tears himself away from his roots at great risk to his future.

But is not this, some may think, a call for a 'head in the sands' philosophy, a romantic and unrealistic retreat away from technology which we abuse yet cannot do without? On the contrary. Without denying the obvious gains of technology, we must become aware that we are creatures of earth, human animals who must, as far as this life is concerned, live in dialogue with the whole of nature. This is more radical than it sounds because we must work out the ethics of man's relationship with his environment. Why should the relationship between man and other creatures be just one way, so that they serve him as his companions, food, and servants? What is man's duty to them? Have they no natural right to enjoy life in their own way? These questions are more momentous than those posed by many today who warn that unless modern man comes to terms with nature humanity is threatened. The latter approach is still dominated by the primacy of man, and it is survival of humanity which is the driving force behind concern at the ecological crisis. The Christian attitude must be bolder than that. As God's creatures we must face squarely the implications that we are in nature and nature is in us, and that this is no small part in our responsibility for the whole of creation as God's stewards. A steward lives from the estate but he does not own it; he may use it but never abuse it. He is, in relationship to it, God's servant and never master.

There is, in fact, a striking relevance about the words uttered by Isaiah so long ago: 'the earth lies polluted under its inhabitants. For they have transgressed the laws and violated the statutes, broken the everlasting covenant. Therefore a curse devours the earth and its inhabitants suffer for their guilt' (24:5-6). The writer was not thinking about an ecological crisis, but he does see a strong connection between a ruined earth and failure of the people to follow God. This is also a Christian perspective. As such, it should be the task of the Christian Church to show the role of nature in God's plan of creation and salvation. Christianity must declare that nature is not merely a backcloth to the drama of salvation, neither is it just man's larder or his sports arena. It is, the Bible asserts, the work of God — good and valuable in his sight. Thus, to exploit and rape the earth is to sin against God himself, whereas to show reverence and love for nature is the proper response of mankind.

(ii) *Man as a moral being.* As one made in the image of God man must face up to the claim of that privilege. As fellow

worker with God he is confronted with the demands of
obedience to the will of God (Gen. 1:28). Relationship to God
always involves moral obligations. So, in the parable of the
Garden prohibitions go with privileges: 'you may eat of every
tree but of the tree of knowledge of good and evil you shall
not eat' (2:17). In reality this command is a great honour to
man. The moral responsibility that is in him is an answering
echo of the moral responsibility that is in God himself, which
is the capacity to act wisely and in love. We note that God
does not face man as tyrant, demanding impossible standards. Freedom is tempered with control — 'every tree but
one' is the command. Man has plenty of choice but it is not
unrestricted. Our modern emphasis upon freedom — 'freedom to do as you please' — is really the charter for chaos and
anarchy. A man does not need to be a Christian to
acknowledge this. Aldous Huxley once said that 'man's worst
difficulties begin when he is able to do as he likes'. Freedom
for moral man is only genuine when he exercises choice in
relationship to God and others. An essential part of man's
uniqueness lies in his ability to respond to God — to run to
him and run from him — as well as his awareness of having
obligations towards fellow humans. 'Thou shalt' awaits the
individual response, 'I choose'. That choice may be the only
moral action possible, but it has to be chosen freely and for
the right motive. All parents know that they can get the right
response merely by offering their children certain incentives
— sweets or other inducements. But no true or abiding
morality can be built on rewards alone. When a child makes
choices for reasons of love and concern for others, sometimes
involving personal cost, we can see that a framework of a
genuine morality is being erected.

Of course modern man is quick to point out that he can be
a moral and responsible being without God, and we would
not wish to deny that man can have real standards without
God. But man needs God to protect himself from man. It is a
strange and ironic quirk that when man is put at the centre of
all, a dehumanising tendency begins; when he is the 'measure
of all things' his value begins to drop. This is well sketched in
Aldous Huxley's fable of the future, *Brave New World*, in
which he explores the nature of a world without God. In this

book the absence of God results in the divinisation of the
community. Man creates man by genetic engineering, and
the individual is graded according to his intelligence and
usefulness to society. Individual aims and happinesses are
subordinated to the well-being of the State. Huxley makes
one of his characters say of the lowest brand of humans, the
Epsilons, 'But in Epsilons we don't need human intelligence...what an enormous saving to the community if the
Epsilon body could be speeded up till it was as quick, say, as
a cow's'. In such a society no one is safe, not even Alpha-plus
beings, because man is graded according to his usefulness and
not according to his status as man; as such there is no dignity
which belongs to man *qua* man. Huxley is really pointing out
that such a 'Brave New World' is a prisoner's nightmare. But
we need no reminders that such a 'utilitarian' view of man
exists outside novels; it is implicitly, and sometimes explicitly,
at the heart of the attitudes of modern totalitarian states
towards humanity. When the State takes the place of God it
makes a cruel and tyrannical master; when Man is glorified,
let the individual beware! But for the Christian, man is of
unique value because it is God who marks up the price,
giving man freedom and dignity.

(iii) *Man as worshipper.* In the two factors above we find the
ingredients of worship. It is true that in the story of Adam
there is no mention of worship as we understand it, but it is
implicit in the response expected of man. Any relationship
which begins with God, demanding obedience, service, and a
close union is worship. Worship is simply giving God his
worth; it is the obligation of gratitude to him. We could say
that it has two main elements, both of which should be
God-directed. The first is that of gratitude expected of
creatures by their Creator, and the second is obedience and
responsibility in all our work. If we are surprised to see 'work'
mentioned as an integral part of worship this is because for
modern man worship has become only a religious duty instead
of a life-time activity. The two elements of gratitude and
work have split off from one another. But an objector might
respond; 'Isn't it rather over-romantic to portray work as part
of man's worshipping activity? After all, think of the monotonous and mundane labour millions of our contemporaries

have to do to earn a few measly dollars; Mrs. Milligan will
have a few picturesque things to say when she is told that her
job in the canteen is part of her activity as a worshipper! In
her eyes her work is connected with keeping little Johnny in a
pair of shoes or helping towards the rent.' Astonishment is
precisely the response we might expect from our contemporaries who fail to see that God's call to man as His image is to
find fulfilment in meaningful and creative labour. Work, in
fact, is not *merely* for slaves, neither is it *merely* a means to an
end; but it is the task assigned by God so that man may
develop according to God's plan, expressing his response
joyfully and freely.

This picture of man whose life is meant to be that of
worship to God has a great deal to say about exploitation of
man in the work situation, as well as about modern man's
perplexity over his work. Let us take one big problem, the
machine, which as a problem has grown steadily in promin-
ence since the industrial revolution. According to many
people it has begun to take over and dominate society.
Thinkers like Lewis Mumford, Jacques Ellul and Theodore
Roszak suggest that modern technology has begun to operate
independently of human values. 'Go,' man said to the
machine, 'be fruitful and multiply and fill the earth and
subdue it and have dominion over the fish of the sea and over
every living thing that moves upon the earth.' And this is
precisely what has happened; the machine has taken over
man's role in the world and has threatened to de-humanise
him. He ends up as a slave of the machine instead of its
master. The machine creates new machines and men fall into
their designated roles as designers, engineers, servicing per-
sonnel, attendants and cleaners; reluctant acolytes of a new
god whose service they dread but whose worship they cannot
withhold. It is called the price of progress, but it has led to the
imprisonment of millions in labour where meaning can no
longer be found. As Sam Keen expressed it: 'homo faber has
become a waste maker, the anus of the machine rather than
its brain.'[7]

Of course we are not advocating a return to a stone-age
culture. Civilisation and industrialisation are proper consequences of the call of God to man to have dominion. But

when man himself is imprisoned by such developments and his true nature distorted by them, it is time to ask 'is humanity being sacrificed on the altar of this idol'? What is needed is to find the correct referent for man's nature and being. We argue that this is only to be found in a doctrine of man which insists on his fundamental obligations to a Creator and Father-God. In place of drudgery, work may become the expression of man's discovery of his value before God and his superiority over machine-culture. Perhaps with this discovery will come the realisation that the whole of life can be offered as worship to God.

MAN AS GOD'S CHILD

How then are we to define the 'image' idea? Our study has led to the conclusion that the designation of man as the image of God has something to do with what he does as well as what he is. One element, we have noticed, is linked to God's command to man to 'have dominion'. To this end he is equipped with reason and will and in this aspect he is like his Creator. But the second section on man's responsibility took us a little further into the meaning — because we saw that it signifies man as a moral, responsible being made for relationship to God and with untold potential for response. So W. Eichrodt remarks: 'For man to be created in the likeness of God can only mean that on him, too, personhood is bestowed as the definitive characteristic of his nature...he is...open to the divine address and capable of responsible action.'[8]

Yet important as this description is of man as a rational and responsible being, we are not satisfied that this exhausts the meaning. The warmth and intimacy of the phrase 'let us make man in our own image' is not captured by such definitions. This indicates that central to the idea is an understanding of man in a warm and intimate relationship with God; a relationship so special that no other creature shares this precious bond. It is not too much to call it a Father-Son relationship which, like all relationships, needs constant fellowship and open contact if it is going to mature into the loving, responsive and permanent associations between God and man. Man is not actually named as God's child in the Genesis narratives but what is there implicitly is worked out explicitly in the rest of Biblical revelation. So the 'image' designates the potential of man called to share the warmth of fellowship with God and life with him. Emil Brunner makes a distinction between man and other creatures in this way: 'figuratively speaking God produces the other creatures in a finished state; they are what they ought to be and this they remain. But God retains man within his workshop, within his hands. He does not simply make him and finish him; human nature, indeed, consists in the fact that we may and must remain in the hands of God.'[9]

But however much the 'image' idea speaks of an internal relationship with God and the promises that follow from this, it also speaks of failure, because this creative process, so potentially great for man, has been interrupted by man's sin that has resulted in an inability to fulfil his nature and commission. Man, called into partnership with God, fails again and again to fufil the hopes that God has pinned on him. Certainly the image of God is in all men, but it is marred by sin and tarnished by lives lived away from his presence. To expand on Chesterton's illustration with which we began this chapter; it is like the man with the lost memory who, let us imagine, has been for years away from home. Anxious to discover his identity, he ransacks his clothes feverishly. He finds clues that describe him but nothing that discloses his true self; a suit from Burtons, a Van Heusen shirt, a few cigarette stubs and coins. The only hope for a man in such a predicament is that a relative might find him, reclaim him and take him back where he belongs. This is exactly what God did in Christ, and that is why the image idea can never be fully understood from the Old Testament alone — it is only from the side of redemption that the idea of man made in God's image becomes part of experience. In Christ the promise becomes fulfilment; and men find what it means to be children of God.

NOTES

1   G. K. Chesterton, *Orthodoxy* (Bodley Head, 1939).

2 H. W. Robinson, *Christian Doctrine of Man* (Edinburgh, 1926), p. 125.
3 J. Passmore, *Man's Responsibility for Nature* (Duckworth, 1974), p. 10ff. and ch. 2.
4 David Jenkins, *What is Man?* (SCM, 1970), p. 75.
5 E. Leach, *Runaway World?* (The Anchor Press, 1968), p. 1.
6 R. Niebuhr, *The Nature and Destiny of Man*, I, p. 179.
7 S. Keen, *Apology for Wonder* (Harper, 1969), p. 135ff.
8 W. Eichrodt, *Theology of the Old Testament*, II (SCM, 1967), p. 126.
9 E. Brunner, *Man in Revolt* (Lutterworth, 1939), p. 97.

CHAPTER 3

Man — God's Problem Child?

AS WE LOOK around at mankind there is much that excites our approval and appreciation. It is a fact we all take for granted that the majority of people do try to live good lives and, by and large, succeed. Many marriages — and these are the ones we do not read about in our newspapers — are lived with honour, faithfulness and love. Millions do live together in peace and harmony. Indeed, the sacrifices made by ordinary people and their devotion to ideals and things of value prompt us to emphasise that there is good in man with enormous potential for growth. We cannot simply brush man aside and label him as 'worthless', 'evil' or 'utterly depraved'. Many of us have arrived at a confidence in humanity because of the way human beings have acted towards us.

While the goodness and decency of man should always be before us, we all realise there is another side to the picture. Rarely is it assumed that human beings are flawless and can live up to their ideals. 'Nobody is perfect,' we say as we make allowances for the follies of others, 'we're all human after all.' We may go further; try as we may to hide behind the veneer of respectability or culture we know that little of fundamental importance separates the cultured city dweller from the primitive tribesman. 'Strip a Spaniard of his virtues,' runs the Spanish proverb,' and you have a Portuguese.' Although this is a wry comment on local rivalry it does point to a real truth about man. Publicly we may give the impression that we are integrated, whole people with few vices — apart from the socially accepted ones! But privately we are aware of an inward war between the opposing drives, ambitions, passions and temptations which are part of ordinary human experience. This aspect of our nature we are anxious to keep hidden from the public eye. Why should others know of our guilt and shame? Will Dyson, an artist on the old London *Daily Herald* once drew a cartoon of an elegant, highly groomed lady meeting Sigmund Freud for the first time. At the end of a rein in Freud's hand was a monstrous ugly ape. 'Allow me,' said the famous psychiatrist, 'to introduce you to your subconscious!' While the Christian would not share Freud's presuppositions concerning the origin of sin and evil there would be unanimity between them on the point that men are never what they seem.

In public life also we have ample evidence of the contradiction in man's nature. 'Everyone has his price,' says the cynic. Perhaps this is nearer the truth than we care to admit. In America the Watergate scandal has shown how men in positions of great responsibility — outwardly very respectable and honest people — can get involved in intrigue, doubletalk, deceit and lies. In Britain also, the Poulson affair of 1973/4 provided the public with another example of the insidious effects of corruption as many well-known leaders in commerce and local government were caught in its net. While society on both sides of the Atlantic condemned such activities, there has been little appreciation of the fact that such behaviour is a manifestation of a poison endemic in man's nature. The 'villains' in these incidents were ordinary respectable people, not élite members of a criminal core.

Explanations of man's plight are not hard to find. The problem of the individual and his inclination towards evil has been the central issue in the longstanding nature-nurture controversy. The 'naturists' who include such diverse thinkers as Hobbes, the Social Darwinists and recent writers like Robert Ardrey, declare that man is a child of his nature and cannot be held responsible for drives which he has inherited biologically. Man is, we agree, a product of nature and is therefore aware of the appetites of the flesh, but while he shares such drives with other creatures he is not at their mercy as they are. He transcends his lowly origins. It will hardly do man justice to make heredity the sole ground for his moral predicament. To remove moral blame from man is in effect to take away what is distinctive about him.

Then there are the 'nurturists' like Locke, Rousseau, T. H. Huxley and Desmond Morris who blame man's evil on to his environment. Rousseau, to his credit, was one of the first to realise the significance of environment upon the development of human nature, but his view, which pivoted upon the goodness of man and the evil of environment, was decidedly unbalanced: 'Man is born free and everywhere he is in chains'. According to him and his followers, a secular heaven will arrive once man is released from the constraints imposed on him by society. But is it true that a man who is free to follow his unrestricted impulses will find true fulfilment? The history of groups seeking emancipation from the tyranny of society does not give us ground for confidence in the view that once man is 'naturalised' he finds Paradise on earth.

The philosophy of Marxism is really another example of the 'nurturist' theme. The individual, according to Marx, is imprisoned by the oppressive commercial and political systems of capitalism. 'Exploited man' can only become free within the framework of a new society. It is society which either liberates or exploits people — so, change society and this will result in changed individuals. Man's ills, then, are social ills. There are many high-minded people today who, while they do not accept Marxism as a political ideology, believe that changes in man's environment will lead to the removal of most of the anomalies in his nature. This, indeed, is the thinking at the heart of current political theory. But this optimism has not been substantiated by improvements in housing, education and social welfare. Without wishing to deny the excellence of many reforms which have undoubtedly alleviated the plight of the needy, we must insist that the problems associated with the nature of man cannot be solved simply by tinkering with his environment. The facts are that in many capitals of the world men and women are not safe to walk freely on the streets after dark; that violence is a spectre that threatens everyone, no longer something confined to the silver screen; that new addictions are taking the place of older ones — such realities shatter the illusion that by improving a man's condition you make him a better man.

Thirdly there is the approach of the *evolutionists* who by combining elements from the nature-nurture debate argue that the problems associated with man's nature will disappear through education and the influence of a rational and humane society. It is sometimes said that there is nothing wrong with man that good will and enlightenment cannot correct; under the guidance of reason man's progress towards wholeness is guaranteed. When events in life appear to contradict the inevitability of progress, proponents of this theory take refuge in separating humanity into two categories — those who are responsible, enlightened people who to some degree foreshadow future man, and those who fall short of this and need education and training. Niebuhr quotes a scientist who, distinguishing between the two classes, stated that 'superman built the aeroplane but ape-man got hold of it'.[1] Moral responsibility is thus conveniently placed at the door of the unenlightened. But as the events of the Second World War showed with such horror the 'superman' vision of Nazism, centred in Nietzsche's dream of freedom based on power, perished with its victims at Auschwitz and Dachau. If the optimism of thinkers who see man's destiny in terms of 'progress' is not yet as dead as the 'superman' concept, nevertheless it is obvious that the history of the last few decades does not bear out their earlier confidence. Against Julian Huxley's noble sentiment that it is 'man's destiny to be sole agent for the future evolution of this planet' we doubt that man can be trusted with such dignity and responsibility when in every area of his life he is divided and alienated. Man has as much resistance to evil as he has to the common cold.

Widespread pessimism therefore persists today concerning the nature of man in spite of the many attempts to explain his predicament. Such a climate may not be very encouraging but it does give credibility to Christian belief that man is a fallen creature. A gloomy doctrine? To some extent, yes, because it hardly pats people on the back. But it has this in its favour, it is realistic and fits the facts as they exist. At the same time it is not a doctrine of despair but contains hope because it is in the sight of God that man is sinful and fallen. The doctrine of sin, in other words, has meaning and

relevance only against the larger and more exciting news of
God's offer of healing.

The Christian faith, therefore, interprets the mystery of
man's divided nature by the idea of his moral obligation and
response to God. He stands before God as a responsible
person and his failure to live according to God's demands is
called 'sin'. We recognise that the word 'sin' has little
meaning for modern people. It appears to come from a past
long dead, when the Church dominated the lives of men
and women, trafficking in souls and priestly absolutions. Now-
adays it may have a fleeting attraction when included in the
title of an 'X-film'. Well, we may get rid of the word if we wish
but we shall still be left with the reality it represents. But sin
in Christian thinking refers not so much to wrongdoing but
rather to a wrong relationship with God which results in evil
actions. Emil Brunner noted correctly that 'sin is never the
beginning; it always comes second. Sin always has a history
behind it'.[2] The idea of man as sinner rests upon the
presupposition that he is a creature made for communion
with God, but now separated from the one in whose image he
is made.

Sin in the Bible

In the Old Testament three words stand out in describing
man's tendency for evil. There is the word '*hattat*' which
means to 'miss the mark' or 'go astray'. When applied to
human experience it pictures sin as a deviation from the right
path so that the sinner is lost. A second word '*awon*' comes
from a verb meaning 'to go aside from the right way'. The
implication is that the wrongdoer leaves the pathway deliberately while being aware of the wrong choice made. A third
term which occurs with great frequency in the prophets is
'*pesha*', often translated 'transgression' but more accurately as
'rebellion'. The first and the third of these words come
together in Job 34:37: 'he addeth rebellion (*pesha*) to his sin
(*hattat*)'.

Although these terms are diverse in meaning there is a
fundamental unity in the Old Testament understanding of
sin seen in part as deviation, crookedness and rebellion. It is

illustrated in many forms in the Old Testament, but none are more profound and more telling than the story of David's evil portrayed with such skill and sensitivity in 2 Sam. 11. The writer shows how because of desire for another man's wife, David schemes the destruction of that relationship, so that he may possess Bathsheba. Lust, deceit, intrigue, adultery and murder are the elements which precede David's conquest. At no point in the affair does David show any conscience, and neither is there any mention of God's approval nor disapproval. Nathan the prophet then comes before David with the apparently innocuous parable of the rich man who owns many sheep, yet covets and steals the only lamb of a poor man. Immediately David's moral sensitivities are aroused, and he leaps to the defence of the poor man with a condemnation of such greed. Nathan interrupts this show of morality with the arresting words: 'You are the man!' With dramatic effect the writer describes David's confusion and contrition as he at last becomes aware that he has transgressed God's standard of holiness.

But where is this standard to be found? The Old Testament provides the answer in the Law (Torah) of God — that blend of ethical standards, religious ritual and judicial prescriptions — which not only declares what is expected of man, but also reveals the holiness of God and his hatred of sin. Contrary to what many believe, the Law given to Moses was not meant to provide a way of salvation, but was given to make clear man's responsibility before God. God's call to man 'be holy for I am holy' (Lev. 11:44) calls man to a standard which, we all know from experience, we fall short of again and again.

The prophets developed the Hebrew understanding of sin in four major ways. First of all they stressed that sin separates a loving God from his people. Hosea, for example, portrays God in human categories; as a lover waiting for his love to return, or like an anxious father waiting for the prodigal to return home (11:1-8). Secondly, they declared the universality of man's sin before God. Isaiah in the temple, seeing the glory of God, becomes not only aware of his own sinfulness, but conscious that his society is guilty as well. Isaiah's picture of the holiness of God is not merely a consciousness of the infinite distance between mortal man and an immortal and transcendent God. It is more fundamental than that — it is an awareness that humanity is diseased in some way and in need of God's salvation. Thirdly, they taught that sin is never a private thing; it always affects others and the life of the community. So Amos attacked those whose insular, selfish 'morality' disturbed the balance of the community. There is in effect no private sin. Fourthly they were critical of the idea prevalent in religious circles that only ceremonial defilement was important to God. 'I hate, I despise your feasts, and I take no delight in your solemn assemblies', is the voice of God through the prophet Amos: 'Take away from me the voice of your songs, to the melody of your harps I will not listen. But let justice roll down like waters and righteousness like an everflowing stream' (Amos 5:21). This kind of preaching shocked and offended the ecclesiastical authorities who had ignored the inner demands of God's Law.

When we move from the Old Testament background into the teaching of Jesus in the Gospels we find there the same acceptance of the reality of sin and its power. He neither speculates about its origin nor explains what he understands by it. Nevertheless, he addressed men and women as 'lost' and in need of God's forgiveness and help. He spoke with clear understanding of the inner nature of man, preaching that sin and evil have their origin in the 'heart' of the individual (Matt. 15:19). Against the idea prevalent then that sinners are special men or groups, he taught that all are involved and all exposed to God's judgment. At the centre of his ministry, therefore, was the appeal for all to 'repent' because in his life and work the Kingdom of God confronted everyone. It is easy to sentimentalise the life of Jesus and convey the impression that he was either a benign counsellor or an over-indulgent social worker. He was neither. The fact is, that Jesus's ministry makes sense only on the basis that man's predicament is grave — that he is lost, enslaved and alienated from God. And the seriousness with which the Bible views the situation is nowhere more clearly shown than in the significance it attaches to the Cross of Christ. It will not do to make this merely an example of sacrificial love; it is, as the Gospels make clear, God's way of dealing with sin.

With this stress Paul is in hearty agreement. In his letter to
the Romans he grapples with the nature of sin and the death
of Christ. Remorselessly and almost clinically he establishes
the fact of universal sinfulness. But how can man 'sin' if he
does not know God's standards of righteousness? Paul
declares that humanity is without excuse. God has revealed
himself plainly in nature and conscience, and it is self-evident
to Paul that the pagan deliberately suppresses the truth he
recognises with his eyes and with conscience. As for the Jew to
whom is given the Torah of God, it is equally certain that he
fails also to keep God's standard of holiness. The indictment,
therefore, against humanity is that: 'All have sinned and
come short of the glory of God' (Rom 3:23). Paul, as a Jew,
knew the keenness of sin as a reality in his life. The Law
which set out the formidable standard of God's hope for man
offered little help, but instead exposed the real depth of man's
helplessness and showed his desperate plight. 'O wretched
man that I am! Who will deliver me from this body of death?'
is the anguished cry of a man aware of the terrifying chasm
which separates him from his God and from true freedom
(Rom: 7.24). It is clear that even in his sin man cannot escape
God. God will not let him go, and his claims are never
withdrawn.

This two-fold revelation of God in creation and through
the Law gives the framework of human responsibility.
Whether he be Jew or Gentile, man holds down the truth; he
uses freedom irresponsibly. The result is that God is removed
from his rightful place in the life of man, and man sets
himself up as God.

Sin and the Fall

As we have seen, the Bible concentrates upon the fact of sin
and makes little attempt to account for its presence in the
world. There is one passage, however, which deserves further
consideration, and that is the description of Adam's expulsion
from the Garden. Genesis 3 expresses in simple terms the
story that God placed man and woman in Paradise with all
things to enjoy, but through the beguilement of the serpent
they disobeyed God and were expelled from his presence.

Toil, pain in child-bearing, death and separation from God, are said to be the fruit of man's wilfulness.

This narrative is passed over by the rest of the Old Testament and is obviously not considered by it to be significant or determinative for the doctrine of man. In the Inter-testamental period, however, speculation developed about the nature of man, leading to wild and outlandish theories concerning Adam's glory, beauty, size, strength and virtue. Contemporary man was seen as but a pale and sad image of the first man, and this decline was due, it was widely believed, to Adam's sin.[3] In the New Testament it is left to Paul to explore the importance of Adam for Christian truth. In Romans he compares Christ's obedience with the disobedience of Adam. 'For if many died through one man's trespass (*paraptoma*)', the apostle states, 'much more have the grace of God and the free gift in the grace of that one man Jesus Christ abounded for many' (Rom. 5:15). In the word 'trespass', meaning a 'slip' or 'false step', the Bible comes closest to the term 'fall' which the early church made the focus for its doctrine of sin.

In the early Church two important interpretations of the fall emerged, both of which influenced later theology. First there was the idea of St. Irenaeus of Lyons (d. 200 A.D.) who visualised Adam, not as a finished and mature being, but as a young creature with unlimited possibilities of growth in relationship with God. The fall occurred when man, so to speak, was in his infancy and weak in his capacity to resist evil. Christ, however, not only healed the breach between God and man but, as the second Adam, continued the progress of man which sin had interrupted. We can see why this theory is popular in contemporary theology because of the ease with which it blends with evolutionary theories. Instead of a tragic vertical fall it offers the suggestion of a providential progress towards a future bright with promise. Irenaeus's view, then, when combined with the idea of evolution treats the fall as an ascent rather than descent; as containing within it a truly human response rather than a tragic, hopeless fall from humanity. By contrast, St. Augustine (354-430 A.D.) on the basis of Paul's argument in Romans 5, together with his own personal experience of the bondage of sin, saw Adam's fall as the great tragedy which for all time taints man's life, action and thought. Mankind is a 'mass of perdition', corrupt and unable to find God unaided — fully deserving God's judgment. This view from one of the greatest thinkers Christianity has ever produced, became until modern times the foundation stone of traditional Christian thinking about man.

But is it really possible for modern people to believe in the 'fall' any longer? Augustine may be excused because he lived long before the rise of the evolutionary theory of man's origins — but surely we today must reject it, whether it be Irenaeus's or Augustine's view, as just a 'fairy tale' of man's plight?

All sane people would reject it were it not for one thing — it is too close to the universal experience of man to receive summary dismissal. G. K. Chesterton once remarked that the teaching about original sin is the one directly ascertainable doctrine of Christianity. There is truth in that statement. Man's nature is in a real sense 'fallen'. We are all aware of a bias towards wrong-doing and conscious of our inability to cope with this inclination towards evil. Frustrated in our attempts to keep the standards we are keenly conscious of, we echo the frustration of Paul, 'the evil I do not want, I do' (Rom. 7:19). Pascal expressed man's dilemma in this way, 'man knows not in what rank to place himself. He has evidently gone astray and fallen from his true place, unable to find it again. Disquieted and unsuccessful, he seeks it everywhere in impenetrable darkness.'[4]

But if we are going to accept some notion of 'fallenness', how is it possible for modern Christians to understand it, while being at the same time faithful to the Bible and modern knowledge? As most of the problems concerning the fall lock into that of the interpretation of the story of Genesis 3, we must return to it again. The crucial question is to decide the main idea that the writer was trying to convey. It is generally agreed that his aim was not to convey scientific knowledge, but to impart spiritual truths about God and man's relationship to him. The narrative is set in a highly figurative and descriptive form, and we lose a great deal if we minimise this framework. So, for example, the serpent is significant only insofar as it symbolises the presence of evil, and the significance of the apple clearly lies not in its 'reality' *qua* apple as in its representation of moral knowledge. Furthermore, the intriguing subtlety of the account is seen in the way the writer uses the word 'Adam' ('man') as both a proper name and as a generic term, oscillating from one to the other. In Gen. 1:26 'Adam' is a generic term standing for mankind and likewise in 2:7. In Gen. 3:17, however, it is a proper name, yet becomes in 3:20 a common noun. In verse 21 it reverts to a proper name again. This oscillation occurs frequently in the following chapters and forces us to ask, is this a deliberate ploy on the part of the writer? It would seem so. If he wished to avoid misunderstanding, all he needed to do was to give the first man a different name. That he did not do so, suggests that he was attempting to convey the timeless significance of mankind lost. Not only did Adam, the first man, sin, but his story is everyman's story. This pattern is found in the Inter-testamental book, the *Apocalypse of Esdras* which asks rhetorically, 'O Adam, what have you done?' and then answers itself, 'but each one is the Adam of his soul'.

This subtle inter-relationship between individual and corporate responsibility is at the centre of Paul's doctrine of sin. Even in that hotly disputed text Rom. 5:12 we may catch a glimpse of Paul's hesitation to blame everything on to Adam. He writes, 'therefore as sin came into the world *through one man* and death through sin, and so death spread to all men because *all men sinned*'. Here Paul is combining two ideas, the first that humanity's fate is inextricably connected with the disobedience of Adam, and the second that sin recurs in varying forms throughout the whole of human life and experience. Paul, it would seem, is aware that to make the sin of one man decisive for all mankind results in a crude form of determinism; thus he views sin as having two foci, in Adam and in each individual. As we saw in the last section, it is an integral part of Paul's argument in Romans that each person, Jew and Gentile, is without excuse.

So, how significant is Adam for Paul? The context indicates that Adam is very significant for Paul's doctrine of salvation but unimportant for his doctrine of sin. In Romans 5 Paul's attention is upon the reality of Christ's victory, and Adam is brought into the argument as the counterfoil, or contrast, to the benefits of salvation. In other words, Paul is explaining Jesus not Adam; he is discussing redeemed mankind not the Adam of Genesis 3. Adam is introduced as a means of showing the significance of Christ. As the antitype of Christ, Adam depicts the dispensation of death and disobedience, yet this palls before the love and triumph of the Cross. Adam and Christ, therefore, contrast each other as representative figures of man's life and death; the one signifying man's lost state, the other signalling the blessings of the new age. All that Christ did and achieved for man is fittingly expressed then in this analogue of the 'last Adam'. Out of man's sin comes a most wonderful and unexpected blessing which puts into the shade the folly and failure of the past. This truth is well expressed in the Paschal liturgy of the Roman Church; 'O happy fault (*O felix culpa*) that merited such a redeemer'.

Our approach to the fall has led us to the conclusion that the Bible's emphasis is not upon the past but the present, not upon origins but upon facts as they are. If we ask the question, 'what has man fallen from?' we must face the puzzle that the Bible says very little about man's Paradisical state. Adam hardly seems to have set foot in the garden before he is out on his ear! There is scarcely a pause between the idea of creation and that of the fall. It would appear therefore that the writer of Genesis does not regard the former state of man as important. It is his present state that dominates his thinking. The value of the Genesis account for the Christian, then, is not that it tells us how and when Adam fell — which it doesn't — but that it describes our nature as sinful beings. 'There is none righteous, no not one' (Rom. 3:10) sums up each of us from first man until last man. The sin of Adam and of everyman affects the lives of others because of our corporate involvement. Every sin is the act of a responsible person and in our disobedience we can blame no one else — yet, as we know only too well, we involve others. Herein lies the paradox of sin — man is guilty and can help it; but he is imprisoned within his own sin, a slave to it and unable to conquer it (John 8:34; Rom. 6:16). How is sin transmitted? Not, as is implied in the Augustinian tradition, by means of seminal transmission. It is not like an heirloom passed down but it is, in John Taylor's words, 'always choice and contagion';[5] it taints and contaminates. Original sin does not, we suggest, merely denote that Adam sinned and involved the world in a dreadful calamity, but that man is ensnared in a web of sin. It comes from his past and pursues him into his future. It starts with 'Adam' and is only defeated by the last Adam.

The doctrine of original sin, of course, is hardly attractive to modern man who does not like the thought of starting off with a handicap, except possibly in golf! It offends his sense of fair play. But what he cannot deny is that it is a devastatingly accurate description of his nature. So Pascal puts it neatly, 'certainly nothing offends us more rudely than this doctrine and yet, without this mystery, the most incomprehensible of all, we are incomprehensible to ourselves'.[6]

The fall of man, therefore, explains man. Its essential message is that man as we encounter him is fallen and is in need of salvation. It tells him that he is estranged from God, imprisoned and helpless within the coils and tangles of his sin. Although we are left with involved questions concerning man's fall, and the daunting mystery of God's purposes in it all, what is given to us is God's diagnosis of our condition. The patient in the consulting room may have many questions concerning his illness — how it was contracted, what is its origin — but at the end of the day all these are secondary to the most pressing question of all, 'how may I get better?' This is the supreme emphasis throughout the Bible; its concern is not on how evil got there, but how it can be conquered.

The Nature of Sin

Sin takes many different forms and it is therefore difficult at first sight to outline the elements common to, say, murder, theft, rape, lying or greed. Questions of motive and the context in which such offences occur, as well as the obvious differences in their nature, serve to further the illusion that they are distinct. In modern law each individual crime is treated separately as it should be, but in the process the relationship of that crime to the nature of evil generally is destroyed. Yet the Christian believes that there are common elements which orchestrate the follies and sin of man, producing not harmony but a monotonous and hideous cacophony.

Inevitably we return to Genesis 3 in our examination of the nature of sin, because here we find the first profound and sustained attempt to analyse its nature.

The first element it highlights is that sin is *rebellion* against God — an act of apostasy in which man dethrones God and substitutes himself. 'You will be like God' says the tempter, 'knowing good and evil' (3:5). The centrality of God is replaced by egocentricity. Yet the fact that man wishes to launch such an attack upon God's citadel requires a prior condition — a breakdown of trust between himself and his maker. The doubt 'has God said?' gives credibility to man's grasp at divinity. In the story there is no doubt that Eve knew that God *had* said, and her willingness to comply with unbelief makes her act of disobedience, and Adam's, quite intentional.

Paul also puts rebellion against the true God at the heart of human sin. Romans 1 echoes the thought of Genesis: 'Claiming to be wise, they became fools, and exchanged the glory of the immortal God for images resembling mortal man...they exchanged the truth about God for a lie and worshipped the creature rather than the Creator' (vv. 23, 25). Here Paul shrewdly puts his finger on the contradiction inherent in man's self-glorification. Man may cast off God to seek freedom, but in so doing he ends up in a cul-de-sac. A child of nature and a child of God, he denies both by becoming the centre of his own world. Man is, as Luther said, *incurvatus in se*, selfishly inclined toward himself. Modern man may congratulate himself on having no need for God, yet it belongs to his nature to find another object for his worship. If he is not following the true God he is busy at the shrine of false gods created after his own likeness. The advantage of the idol, however, is that it makes no absolute claim and man can manipulate it for his own ends. Luther's apt phrase, '*Der Mensch hat immer Gott oder Abgott*' (man always has either God or idol), goes to the heart of man's dilemma; the very existence of man demands a centre around which he organises his life. In his larger Catechism Luther develops this theme, 'that to which your heart clings and entrusts itself is really your God'. But what are modern-day idols? They are too numerous for accurate survey. They would include commonplace things like money, television, sport, career, family, house, one's looks, and so on. A man's god is that for which he lives, that which excites and absorbs him, that which controls his interest and concern. In Paul's opinion such worship of self or idol results in depravity and foolishness: 'claiming themselves to be wise they become fools' (Rom. 1:22). In Kierkegaard's view the result of rejecting God involves man in rejecting himself, a form of death wish. 'The murder of God,' he exclaimed, 'is the most dreadful form of suicide.'[7]

A second element in sin is *pride*. In his great book *The Nature and Destiny of Man*, Reinhold Niebuhr distinguished between three types of pride: power, knowledge and virtue. Man's pride in power and his lust for it often take very sinister and terrifying forms. When embodied politically in a national form it takes on a form of 'divine right' to govern, without any appeal to the Divine. Nazism was a dreadful example of such an absolute system which took the place of God and demanded total worship, recognising no morality and no appeal beyond the framework of its own system. Marxism shows the same symptoms and the same exclusive character. Life, people, freedom become subordinated to ideological goals — the contingent 'means' to absolute 'ends'. But the individual may also sell his soul to the desire for power. The desire to possess other people, to tyrannise them and own them, is not unknown in the modern world; and in Christian thought it is another example of man playing at being God.

Pride of knowledge is a more subtle and plausible form of idolatry. We are all aware of the importance of knowledge; scientific research after all is the basis for man's control of his environment and the stupendous progress in technology over the last few decades. But a society may make 'Science' or a particular branch of knowledge the final and ultimate arbiter of truth. As a result a form of materialism may emerge as the touchstone of a society, leading to extreme scepticism regarding all spiritual values — not that such values have been examined objectively, but because of the assumption that scientific judgments are objective, impersonal and supreme over all other forms of understanding reality. Now the Christian has no cause to attack knowledge, which he believes is God-given anyway, but he does repudiate its misuse and elevation into another '*Abgott*'. In Christian theology man's intellect shares in the 'fallenness' of man, not in the sense that it is crooked, but that because man's nature is self-orientated his so-called objectivity is very questionable indeed. The destruction of the myth of total scientific neutrality and objectivity, by such thinkers as Polanyi and Kuhn, comes as no surprise to the Christian who has always believed that knowledge is dependent upon God and ultimately worthless away from him.[8] Proverbs rightly points out that 'the fear of the Lord is the beginning of wisdom and the knowledge of the Holy One is insight' (1:7).

Thirdly, there is the pride in virtue or self-righteousness. Who has not known this insidious temptation? It is perhaps the most evil of all forms of pride because it identifies itself with God's standard, assuming that one's own estimate of good deeds, good life, good reputation is also accurate in God's sight. It is not only Jews who stand condemned by Paul's remarks that 'they have a zeal for God, but not according to knowledge. For they, being ignorant of God's righteousness and going about to establish their own, have not submitted to the righteousness of God' (Rom. 10:2, 3). Ironically, goodness itself was at the heart of the failure of the Jewish people to hear and heed God's message. They assumed that, because *they* were convinced they were good people, God must share that opinion also; the net result was that their claim to be righteous became a barrier to God's message. We need to remind ourselves as well as others that although morals are an integral part of the Christian faith they are never the basis of it. The defence put up by so many good people that 'I've never done anybody any harm' is evasion, a retreat into self-justification. Christianity begins when evasion and self-deception peter out in confession. Niebuhr expressed it admirably: 'the sinner who justifies himself does not know God as judge and does not need God as saviour.'[9] Self-deception accompanies all attempts to avoid the presence of God. Take the case of the morally upright man who points the finger at others like the Pharisee in Jesus's parable: 'God,

I thank thee that I am not like other men...or even like this tax-collector' (Luke 18.11). The persistence of this form of evasion is brought out in John Baillie's story of the sunday school teacher who ended a lesson on that parable with the words 'and now, children, let us thank God that we are not as that Pharisee'![10] Recognition that we' are the 'Pharisee' in question becomes the moment of real self-discovery and healing, because that is the only place God starts from.

The Result of Sin

Sin results in three things; alienation from God, frustration within the individual, and disruption in his relationships.

According to the Bible the effect of sin is destruction of the relationship between God and man. This is dramatically symbolised in the story of Adam hiding from the presence of God. Ashamed and guilty, he must avoid God, yet, paradoxically, in his sin he is conscious now of a new aspect of God which had not hitherto been revealed, that is, his holiness and purity. Formerly it had been his privilege to share the warmth, love and fellowship of God — now this is forgotten as sin widens the distance between them. This sad tale is echoed in the experience of every man. To the man who rejects God, God is present in his holiness and man avoids confrontation with him. Perhaps this sheds light on the obstacles that the gospel of Jesus Christ meets in society. Christians are sometimes surprised that their message — even when it is put over with charm, tact and persuasiveness — is met by embarrassment or avoidance. It appears to make people uncomfortable and is news that they want to avoid at all costs — anything but hear that they are sinners and that God loves them and wants them! But, of course, this reaction is the instinctive recoil of the 'natural' man who does not want to know his true state before God, and at the superficial level does not care two raps about sin. He thinks he can live with it and even enjoy it — as long as God is not about! However, the consequence of sin according to the scriptures is not only that the relationship between God and man is damaged but also that man is now under God's wrath and under his just sentence; 'the wages of sin is death' (Rom.

6:23). The Law consequently, God's standard of holiness, becomes for man a burden and a curse as its demands become an impossible goal for him to fufil. Try as he may to pull himself up by his bootlaces, he stumbles and falls. Prostrate and helpless he hears the condemnation, 'the wrath of God is revealed against all ungodliness and sin' (Rom. 1:18).

But doesn't this run counter to the idea that God is love? Is it really credible that God should condemn men to eternal damnation for their foolish and rather trivial offences? Such questions fail to take into account the true nature of God's love. Love is so sentimentalised these days that it scarcely means more than a vague tenderness and benevolence for others. But God's love is holy love. It expresses itself not by compromising with sin — which is the modern way — neither by condoning it, but by condemning *and* dealing with it. God's holy love intervenes, not like a 'preemptive strike' which destroys both sin and sinner, but in such a way that the root cause of sin and evil is destroyed and the sinner saved. This is the work of the Cross. And strange as it may seem, it is only in the light of a doctrine of sin which takes into account God's hatred of sin, that we can appreciate the wonder of his love; 'to whom much is forgiven, the same loves much' said Christ (Luke 7:47). Only from the side of redemption can we appreciate the extent of God's enduring compassion for men.

Sin also brings frustration to the individual. The quest for self-gratification leads not to fulfilment, as is intended, but to dissatisfaction. Somehow, at the very point of achieving what we desire, we find frustration, because what once seemed so exhilarating and rewarding is now strangely empty and stale. It is almost as if the invisible chains of sin tie man down to one level of existence, so that the things he needs he doesn't want, and the things he wants do not satisfy. As guilty people we experience in our sin the meaning of alienation. So Kierkegaard confesses 'How man fell I do not know; why men fall I now know within myself.' And St. Augustine, that self-taught analyst of human sin, probed the feeling of helplessness known to us all: 'many sins are committed through pride but not all proudly...they happen, so often through ignorance, by human weakness; many are committed by men weeping and groaning in their distress.'[11] Perhaps nowhere is this sense of frustration more acutely felt than in man's dread of death. Aware of his mortality, man is filled with fear of the future because he has no security in anything other than himself. His nature cries out for immortality, but death sweeps him into the blackness below. There is a strong emphasis in the Bible on the fact that man without God cannot face death confidently. He may place his trust in the present moment but has no firm hope beyond this existence.

We may trace the disruption created by sin in community life as well. Our experience shows us daily how evil infects society, spreading from one person to another, alienating brother from brother and community from community. We know only too well that evil moves faster than love and has a much greater fascination for us all. In Morris West's novel *The Tower of Babel* Franz Liebermann comments on the problem of evil in the world in this way: 'We are still children squabbling over an apple, tearing at each other, while the apple lies filthy in the dust.' Perhaps there is a subtle glance at the story of the fall. The fact remains that the 'dust' — to use Morris West's term — is so much a part of the texture of human living that we find it difficult to focus our minds on the nature of sin. It is such a constituent of life that we find life difficult to understand or imagine without it. We take it into our reckoning constantly. It is not surprising that most of man's ambitions for the reform of society and visionary dreams for a transformed Utopian community end up in practice as mere tinkering with external matters or repair-work. What is needed most desperately of all is a radical transformation of society at the level of every individual. The attempt to create an Eden after the fall is at best mistaken idealism, and at worst folly.

So we have seen that man, in relation to God, to others, and in himself, is divided and frustrated. Hardly an attractive picture, but we must point out that this does not imply that men are as totally depraved or as wicked as they possibly can be. Neither should we exaggerate the evil of sin above the greatness of God's love. Jonathan Edwards, a preacher and theologian in the eighteenth century, used the doctrine of total depravity to teach that every child born into the world is more hateful to God than the most loathsome viper that crawls! A contemporary, however, commented that 'neverthe-less, Edwards seemed to have a very happy time of it in the midst of eleven little vipers of his own begetting!'[12] This discrepancy between his theology of sin and love for his own children suggests that Edwards' theory hardly does justice to the character of God, or indeed to the true nature of man. Although all are sinners not all share the same degree of guilt. If the idea of total depravity means that all men everywhere are as bad as they can be the idea is a blatant and obvious untruth. However, in orthodox Christian circles it has not usually had this meaning. It does not mean that men are essentially wicked, but that sin extends to the whole of their nature. Thus the idea expresses the extent of sin, not its depth. The whole of human existence is permeated by the consequences of the severed relationship between God and man. Sin, because it is at rock bottom a violation of love, leads to man's failure to fulfil his full potentiality. Spiritually helpless, he cannot achieve the destiny for which he was created, neither can he love God from the heart — try as he may. Because he is morally weak, even the observation of a high code cannot bring peace of mind, as Luther discovered from his long years as an Augustinian monk. Divided within, his nature can only be fully integrated if God intervenes to help him.

NOTES

1 R. Niebuhr, *The Nature and Destiny of Man*, I, p. 100ff.
2 E. Brunner, *Revelation and Reason* (SCM, 1947), p. 26.
3 See W. D. Davies, *Paul and Rabbinic Judaism* (SPCK, 1962), ch. 2.
4 B. Pascal, *Pensées* (Penguin Classics, 1966), 400.
5 *Man in the Midst* (Highway Press, 1955), p. 31.
6 *Pensées*, 131.
7 S. Kierkegaard, *Christian Discourses* (London, 1939), p. 70.
8 M. Polanyi, *Personal Knowledge* (Routledge and Kegan Paul, 1958). T. S. Kuhn, *The Structure of Scientific Revolutions* (University of Chicago, 1962).
9 R. Niebuhr, *The Nature and Destiny of Man*, I, p. 213.
10 *Invitation to a Pilgrimage* (OUP, 1942), p. 60.
11 *De Natura et Gratia*, XXIX, 33.
12 S. Doniger (ed.), *The Nature of Man* (Harper, 1962), ch. 2.

CHAPTER 4

Paradigm Man

ONE OF THE classic themes of Western films is that of the small Western town terrorised by a band of gunmen who shoot it up, steal, dominate, and hold everyone at their mercy. When things are at their blackest one of the townsfolk, up to this moment as ordinary, as helpless, and as insignificant as the rest, buckles on his gunbelt to fight evil. Tension mounts as he takes on the gunmen one by one, until finally the story reaches the climax every boy loves: hero and gang leader meet in the High Street. They draw. Our hero is wounded — but the villain bites the dust. This kind of story appeals to all of us. That is how good should and ought to triumph over evil. We all desire that good should be seen to be victorious so that meaning and common sense prevail in the world.

Christianity is at once similar to, yet dissimilar from, that symbol-myth. It states, as we have seen, that the world is one in which man has failed. He has fallen short of his own human nature and destiny and is in bondage to the powers of evil and sin. Unable to do anything about it he looks for help in an apparently hopeless situation. Yet the dissimilarity lies in the fact that Jesus, the centre of the Christian drama, instead of conquering the powers of evil, is 'driven out of town' to a most ignominious death. Good appears to suffer a most crushing defeat. To the outsider, the claim of the Christian Church that the death of Jesus is, in fact, victory is a black joke.

The scandal of Christianity is indeed not new. It was there

from the outset. The claim of the Christians that the crucified 'criminal' was the promised Messiah of God was to the Jews a most horrifying, blasphemous statement. And the claim that Jesus brought meaning to the Universe was to the ever-questioning Greeks foolishness of the most laughable kind. Paul summarised the objectionable nature of Christianity in his bold statement that 'we preach Christ crucified, a stumbling block to the Jews and folly to Gentiles' (1 Cor. 1:23). From a human point of view it is natural to find Christianity a scandal. After all, if we were going to invent a religion we would do a better job than that! We wouldn't build one with so many handicaps: a Jew, that's bad enough, but a Jew from Galilee — an artisan from a Judaean backwater — born in very suspicious circumstances, a so-called miracle worker who died on a cross as a criminal, and said to be risen from the dead! The embarrassments within the story may be seen from the fact that when Christianity began to spread quickly in the early centuries, some pagan philosophers in the court of the Emperor Severus were commanded by the Emperor's wife, Julia Domna, to copy the story of Jesus without its scandalous elements! So they concocted a story based on the Gospel, around the life of a first century philosopher, Apollonius of Tyana, but one that avoided the humiliating fact of crucifixion. In this pagan version of the 'Gospel' Apollonius is triumphantly transferred from trial to heaven.

There are in fact two basic questions concerning Jesus Christ which appear to present fundamental barriers to belief. The first is expressed like this: 'Christianity makes the man Jesus the centre of everything. But why Jesus? Why make an extraordinary fuss about him when Socrates, Plato, Julius Caesar and Karl Marx stand out as men who also influenced history?' The second question ties up closely with the first. Our questioner asks: 'I can admire Jesus as a man and there is much of value in Christianity, but I cannot go along with the mythological assumption that his life and death have some significant purpose with cosmic conse-quences.' These questions need to be kept uppermost in our minds and it is hoped that in the course of this chapter answers to them will emerge.

The enigma of Jesus

Although Christianity is centred on Jesus of Nazareth it doesn't begin there. As we have seen already, it really begins with God, the Creator and Father of all, who loves his creatures even though they have rebelled against him. God is seen as the merciful one who chooses a people for himself in order to redeem the world and to bring it under his Lordship. But even in this choice of a people God acts with inexplicable discrimination. He by-passes great empires such as Egypt and Babylon; he ignores the brilliant culture of Greece; and chooses instead a rabble of slaves in Egypt. Upon this motley company of people called 'Israel' he pours his love; chastening, rebuking, caring and teaching her to serve him as a kingdom of priests and a holy nation. Out of Israel's failure to fulfil her destiny, the expectation began to emerge that God himself would send someone to redeem his mankind — one who would bring healing, life, joy and freedom where there is sickness, death, sadness and bondage.

The absolute claim of Christianity is that this hope is fulfilled in Jesus. Indeed, Christianity claims itself to be what no other religion has ever claimed: the living expression of God's entry into mankind. It asserts that God became incarnate (that is, made of flesh, or made man) in Jesus of Nazareth. Of course, the Christian faith has never pretended to be able to define exactly what this means, but it is committed to the belief that Jesus disclosed God to such an extent that the confession that he is 'God' is the only proper Christian response (John 20:28). Although the idea of Jesus as one who reveals the nature of God is in keeping with the messianic hope of the Old Testament, the significance of Jesus transcends this background. The Old Testament, indeed, looks ahead longingly to the one who would redeem, but the picture it gives of the Messiah is by no means clear. Perhaps of more importance for the understanding of Jesus is the implicit awareness of the Old Testament that man, made in God's image, belongs to God and is in a real sense God's child. Human nature, therefore, becomes a fit vehicle for the manifestation of the divine, even though to our understanding the incarnation is a most staggering and humbling idea.

But, of course, it is only from the vantage point of faith that Jesus is considered to be of special importance. It is the believing Church that makes the great confession that 'Jesus is Lord.' The New Testament itself is written from the standpoint of faith, in that it expresses the confession of the infant Church that 'God spoke to our fathers by the prophets, but in these last days he has spoken to us by a Son' (Heb. 1:2). This admission is very revealing because it shows that those who wrote the New Testament and those who read the documents knew Christ, not only as a person of some significance, but as one who had transformed their attitude to the world around. It is, we must acknowledge, quite extraordinary for writers — even ancient writers — to speak of a near contemporary as 'master', 'lord', 'saviour', 'logos' and so on. The fact that this was done by Jews, with their sturdy belief in the transcendence and unity of God and in the immutability of his Law, make the statements of the New Testament very remarkable indeed and worthy of study. But when Jesus began his ministry it was not immediately obvious that he was of any great importance. What were the factors that made him stand out and that led to that kind of response?

The evidence of the New Testament, when it reports the life and ministry of Jesus, is of a person who did not fit into the categories of contemporary thinking. It is highly likely that people at first regarded him as an ordinary rabbi. But if a rabbi, he spoke and acted in a most un-rabbinical way! Not only was he highly critical of the religious practices and standards of his day, but he also condemned the way the Law was being interpreted by the rabbis and those in authority. He did not deny the divine origin of the Law or indeed its relevance, but he did attack the application and misuse of it. What was more, whereas the rabbi would bow to the authority of the Torah and make it his life's work to expound it and reveal its secrets, Jesus acted as if it were the role of the Torah to expound and reveal Him! He spoke as if he fulfilled the Law and transcended it: 'You have heard it said...but I say unto you' (Matt. 5:21, 27 etc.).

To many more of his observers Jesus may have appeared as a prophet; like the prophets of old he came with a message which spoke of the consequences of disobedience and of the issues of life and death. But once again it is difficult to keep Jesus in this category. Unlike the prophet who came with a vision or a revelation from God to which the prophet was bound, Jesus's authority is unrestricted and resides in himself. That he is superior to the categories of rabbi and prophet is the implication of the story of the Transfiguration, where Moses and Elijah, representing the law and the prophets, are seen as having their fulfilment in the ministry of Jesus.

If it is difficult to fit Jesus into the compartments of rabbi and prophet, it is equally difficult to confine him to any category of Old Testament speculation. The impressive quality of his life and deeds made people want to classify him as the Messiah. Messianic expectation flourished at the time of Jesus and a great variety of different portraits of the expected Messiah existed, according to the needs and predilections of the various Jewish sects. Within Palestine the hope was for one who would lead God's people into victory from oppression and who would set up a Kingdom based on Jerusalem. This type of expectation was clearly nationalistic and exclusive. Now it is quite obvious that a great number of people saw in Jesus the nexus of many of the traits necessary for a messianic leader. His leadership qualities, charismatic appeal, his fire and passion for God, together with his call for the establishment of God's kingdom, all made him a focus for the wistful messianism of his day. But it was a role he refused to perform in spite of the pressure. Although others used the term 'messiah' of him, he persistently avoided it as a self-designation. Even when it is applied to him at Caesarea Philippi (Mark 8:27ff) he made it quite clear to his bewildered disciples that he had a different idea of the Messiah from theirs — one in which suffering replaces glory; indeed, in God's book it is glory.

How, then, do we decode the mystery of Jesus? Who was he and what did he stand for? How may he be our contemporary today? It is the clear conviction of the New Testament that Jesus can only be understood in the context of two fundamental and opposing ideas: the love and justice of God, and the sinfulness of man. Place Jesus in any other context and he becomes incomprehensible. The claim of the New Testament is that the uniqueness of Jesus lies in representing man to God and God to man. This, it argues, is the main aim and purpose of his life.

Jesus is the revelation of what man should be

That Jesus was man is the clear testimony of the Gospels. Nothing in his life stood out to make others think there was anything abnormal about his manhood. For the main part of his life he existed as an ordinary individual in the village of Nazareth. Although obviously we have no clues as to what happened during those 'hidden years', certainly his own family were in no doubt about his real humanity. Later apocryphal gospels tended to glorify the youthful Jesus as a rather brash, precocious 'god' but we may safely regard such accounts as fabrications of the truth. Neither, indeed, during his ministry was there any dramatic revelation that he was anything other than man. Whatever titles were given to him, however incisive his teaching, and however wonderful his deeds, he was treated as a human being with the same feelings as anyone else. The difference between Jesus and other men was not seen, to begin with, as a difference between divinity and humanity but between an authentic human existence and something unauthentic. Jesus lived a human life that appeared to fulfil the longings and desires of others. This is the impression conveyed by the New Testament. The impact of Jesus, in fact, lay in two directions: in his teaching he aroused men to realise their human predicament, and in his life he attracted men to a fulfilment of their humanity.

First of all in his teaching and ministry he revealed what man is existentially — sinful, alienated from God and divided in his nature. He spoke to the deepest needs of people. To those burdened by sin and guilt he gave release through the authority that resided in him, and because of this encountered the hostility of those who considered he was usurping God's role (Mark 2:7). To those who looked for God's redemption he spoke of fulfilment (Matt. 11:4-6). To those who were the victims of the divisions within society — the

children, women, slaves, weak and sick — he showed his
gentleness and compassion (Mark 1:29, 32, 41). But this was
no 'milksop' Messiah; he was trenchant in his attack on the
hypocrisy of his religious contemporaries. From the outset of
his ministry he made implacable enemies by his firm and
unflinching stand for integrity, honesty and goodness (Mark
2:8, 17; 3:6 etc.). All these features of his ministry, and more,
found their focus in his teaching about the Kingdom of God
which, he claimed, was present in his ministry. Of course, for
the Jew the idea of the Kingdom of God (*malkuth shamayim*)
was not new; but in the teaching of Jesus it now takes on a
new and exciting form. It is a Kingdom open to all who turn
to God in repentance, open to all those who, in the eyes of the
righteous, do not by 'right' belong to it (Matt: 23:13, 7:7). A
Kingdom of which Jesus himself is the key. In his deeds and
in his words the Kingdom has already begun. A man's
relationship to Jesus determines his relationship to God and
whether or not he belongs to the Kingdom.

But secondly, and of equal importance, Jesus revealed in
his life what man is in essence, or, to put it another way, what
he is meant to be. We could call him the fully integrated
man. In spite of all the forces and pressures upon him he
shows an amazing capacity to remain whole and at peace. As
a human being he must have known the lure of sin and its
many forms. The New Testament Jesus is not a docetic
Christ, unruffled and unmoved by temptation because of his
essential divinity. Jesus, to be one with us, must have known
temptations to doubt, sexual temptations, temptations of fear
and even the temptation of wishing to play the Creator. But
to be tempted and to know it in all its intensity is not the
same as to sin. Here we must dispute with Kierkegaard who
argued that to be tempted is to sin because it proceeds from
'anxiety which is the psychological condition which precedes
sin.'[1] But with respect to Kierkegaard, he has failed to see the
Biblical context of temptation. Temptation is not something
that one can bypass; it is part of the nature of man. It affects
everyone, including Jesus, who, by virtue of the fact that
he shares our nature, is open to the forces of temptation. In
his life Jesus knew of the enticements of sin but faced
them victoriously throughout his life and grew to complete

manhood as a result. The writer to the Hebrews draws
attention to the tension between growth and perfection:
'although he was a Son he learned obedience through what
he suffered, and being made perfect he became the source of
eternal salvation to all who obey him' (Heb. 5:8). Significantly, Jesus himself never makes the claim that he was sinless. It
is his friends and contemporaries who were struck by the
perfection of the life of their friend and teacher, and they
marvelled: 'here is a man, tempted in all ways as we are, but
free from sin's power and corruption' (Heb. 4:15; 2 Cor. 5:21;
1 Pet. 2:22). No one could throw stones at him on account of
his way of life. 'I find no fault in him', was Pilate's puzzled
reaction to the charges brought against Jesus at his trial, but
it could equally be applied to every area of his life. We could
say, and this is the positive side of the doctrine of sinlessness,
that he 'practised what he preached'. The daunting standard
of the Sermon on the Mount taught by Jesus as a framework
for Christian living must have also been the framework of his
life. Indeed the one who also said 'be perfect (*teleios*, meaning
wholeness or completeness) as your heavenly Father is perfect'
(Matt. 5:48) was either a cool hypocrite or someone who
manifested this wholeness in his whole life. It is impossible, as
Emil Brunner said, 'to discover any hiatus between his
teaching and his person.'[2]

Jesus also stood out in his 'openness' to others. It expressed
itself in various ways. At one level it showed itself in a life of
integrity in which no double standards were at work. During
the Watergate crisis Gerald Ford was appointed Vice-
President in place of Spiro Agnew. The appointment of this
fairly ordinary politician won wide acceptance. Why? The
Sunday Times put it down to one factor — integrity. The
article continued, 'His greatest asset is that he is believed
instantly.'[3] Perhaps no greater words could ever be used of a
public figure than that. But Jesus was that kind of man.
Hypocrisy and cant had no place in the life of Jesus as may
be seen in his dealings with people. Individuals could be
themselves in his presence because he was reliable and would
not let them down. It is to be seen most of all in his sensitivity
and care for others. If the pop song is correct in its assertion
that 'love is surrender' then we can certainly see love in Jesus's

surrender of himself to others. He becomes vulnerable in his openness to help and heal and in his willingness to identify with the suffering and oppression of others. It is little wonder that the human Jesus has become a symbol to men in every age in their longing for deliverance from bondage and oppression, because to live sacrificially for others and die for them wins the admiration of us all. In short, he lived out perfectly the full implications of the word *agape* — love. Love is a devalued word today but it is still instantly identifiable. If we were asked to produce an identikit of a good person, love would be at the top of the qualities mentioned. Jesus's life is, indeed, an *agape*-life. He lived love, and he made his way of love a pattern for others. In that great acted parable of John 13 he took a bowl and towel and washed the feet of his astonished friends. Then he said, 'You call me teacher and Lord; and you are right, for so I am. If I, your teacher and Lord, have washed your feet you also ought to wash one another's feet. For I have given you an example (*hypodeigma*) that you also should do as I have done to you' (vv. 13-15). The word translated 'example' really means a pattern or model. In today's idiom we might say that in this acted symbol we have the breath-taking life-style of Jesus; the pattern of his humanity which is the model for all who claim to follow him. To be with Jesus is to enter an environment of love which in terms of its commitment to others is costly and demanding. D. H. Lawrence once shrewdly observed, 'Hate is not the opposite of love. The real opposite of love is individuality.' Christ's life was a self-giving life for others because he worked through the consequences of love.

All the evidence concerning Jesus leads in one direction, that he was open to all the possibilities and demands of life, yet living and acting a human existence selflessly and freely. It is, of course, self-evident that he could only be 'The Man' if he were 'a man' — but the life he lived forces us to exclaim: 'What a man!'

Jesus as Adam

It is important to realise that this idea that Jesus is true man, revealing in his life what human existence may become, is not a secondary element within the New Testament but an integral part of the gospel itself. The *whole* life and ministry of Jesus, not just his passion and death, is of the utmost significance for the Christian faith. It is a mistake to make his death the only focus of his atonement and to ignore the breadth of his incarnation. This tendency has been common in Protestant theology with the result that the life of Jesus has been treated as a rather pleasant preamble to his work on the Cross. 'The Atonement is the significant content of the Incarnation,' correctly observed Niebuhr, thus uniting the two elements.[4] To ignore the significance of Christ's life leads to a split between the doctrine of creation and that of redemption because the idea of Jesus as man is lost. Thus, we argue, Jesus's whole ministry must be understood from the viewpoint that he is true man, true Adam, whose mission is to reunite an alienated world with its maker. Let us, then, consider three elements in the New Testament where the Adam story is in the background forming a fitting contrast to Christ's work of salvation.

1. The temptations

The baptism of Jesus which heralded the start of his ministry was followed at once by the temptations of Jesus. This was, of course, not the first or indeed the last time Jesus experienced temptation, but these particular trials take us right to the heart of Christ's work. The fact that all the synoptic Gospels mention these wilderness experiences indicate their pivotal importance (Mark 1:12; Matt. 4:1-11; Luke 3:21-22). There are differences between the accounts, but they are not sufficient to affect the importance or meaning of the incident. We notice first of all that the story is all about a confrontation between the devil and the man Jesus at the start of his work. Like the first Adam the ministry of Jesus is full of promise. It is significant that the last recorded dialogue between man and evil occurred in the garden in Genesis 3. Now the second Adam faces the temptations of evil in the wilderness which the garden has become. As in the garden so now the devil begins by questioning the reliability of God's word. 'This is my beloved son,' is the heavenly cry at the

baptism, but the tempter implies a doubt. 'If you are the son
of God.' This is not significantly different from the serpent's
insinuation in Genesis 3: 'Did God say?' In both cases there is
a subtle attack on the basis of the relationship between God
and Adam. Once the trustworthiness of God is in doubt, the
way is open for man to follow his own desires. So Christ is
urged to make bread, an obvious test of the authenticity of
the assurance that this is my 'beloved son'. Jesus, of course, is
well aware that something far deeper than food is involved in
the temptation; that is, the basis of his obedience and trust in
God. And his reply goes to the heart of the temptation: 'Man
shall not live by bread alone but by every word that proceeds
out of the mouth of God.' Although God's son, he does not
retreat into the security of the relationship but he replies that
man's true life consists not in self-aggrandisement but obedience to God, the giver of life. The next two episodes
emphasise the temptation to use the divine power in him to
unwarranted ends. In the second temptation the devil cajoles
him that to leap off the temple roof, and thus precipitate an
angelic rescue act, would confirm his messianic claim and
lead to immediate acceptance by all. Unmoved by this
temptation to achieve instant recognition as God's chosen
one, Jesus is given a glimpse of the kingdoms of the world and
promised possession of them all — if he submits to the devil.
With the words, 'You shall worship the Lord your God and
him only shall you serve,' Jesus put an end to the conflict; the
power entrusted to him was God's power and must be used as
God directs. Jesus stands, then, in sharp contrast to Adam,
who misused his freedom to acquire god-like independent
power, and in so aspiring came into bondage.

2. The Son of man

The obedience and humility which marked the life of Jesus
is symbolised in the term which Jesus deliberately adopted to
express his ministry, namely that of 'son of man'. Uncertainty
still revolves around the significance of the term for Jesus and
his contemporaries, but it is generally agreed that one of the
meanings carries the overtones of a representative manhood.
This is suggested not only by the etymology of the term in

that the Aramaic 'Bar-nasha' means 'man' in contrast to God, but also by reference in Dan. 7:13, 18 where the 'son of man' represents the 'saints of the most High'. Jesus may then have chosen this title not only because of its enigmatic quality but perhaps because its meaning involves a strong corporate element. So the son of man represents all men and shares in their weakness; identified with the lot of Adam, he comes to suffer and save. Whereas the first Adam chose the pathway of *hubris* the second and last Adam walks the path of humility and obedience. The New Testament, far from merely suggesting that this man Jesus was a dutiful visual aid of what man was intended to be, is asserting that he takes up the battle for man against the power of sin and evil, conquering them by his perfect obedience and matchless sacrifice. Jesus, in fact, is not new man but true man. His humanity is not different from ours, as we saw earlier. The relevance of Jesus to mankind demands that his humanity should be the same as ours. He enters into a sinful world and shares the fallen conditions of a human life with the exception of sin. It is not surprising that Paul hesitates a little and ends up in a little confusion when he describes Christ as being 'sent in the likeness of sinful flesh' (Rom. 8:3). Paul, like us, found the incarnation a mysterious and wonderful fact. He could not deny the humanity of Jesus, Son of David (Rom 1:1) born of a woman (Gal. 4:4) but Christ's entrance into sinful humanity leads him to say 'likeness' so that Christ's sinlessness is preserved. Elsewhere Paul does not flinch at demonstrating Christ's full identification with mankind (Rom. 9:5; 2 Cor. 5:16; Gal. 4:4). Irenaeus later takes up the same theme of Christ's involvement in man's fight against sin and evil: 'as through man conquered, our whole race went down into death, so through man conquering we might ascend into life.'[5] Irenaeus was the first Christian thinker outside of the New Testament to see the significance of Jesus as second Adam, as one who is involved in all the dramas and tragedies of life so that his love and salvation may penetrate. So he writes: 'He passed through every age, becoming an infant for infants, thus sanctifying infants — a child for children...being at the same time an example of piety, righteousness and submission...a youth for youths and likewise an old man for old men.'[6] We may find such language strange and a little far-fetched, especially the bit about 'an old man for old men', but what we do not deny is the insight that in Jesus, the second Adam, human nature was most fully and deeply realised.

3. Obedient Man

It is Paul, of course, in the New Testament, who makes the close parallel between Adam and Christ. In Romans 5:12-21 he contrasts the benefits of Jesus with the effects of Adam's fall. Whereas Adam through disobedience involved others in the ensuing alienation, Christ's act of obedience leads to righteousness and life. The death of Jesus in this passage is seen not on its own as a solitary act of obedient sacrifice to the will of God, but as the final act of sacrifice to crown a life of obedience. These ideas are echoed in that familiar passage in Philippians 2:5-11. One of Paul's objectives in writing the letter to the Philippians was to deal with the problem of rivalry and self-assertiveness in the Church. Paul, probably utilising a contemporary hymn, reminds the Christian believers in Philippi of the example of Christ.

> Have this mind among yourselves
> which you have in Christ Jesus,
> Who, though he was in the form of God,
> did not count equality with God
> a thing to be grasped
> but emptied himself, taking
> the form of a servant...

A remarkable piece of literature, and an outstanding snatch of theology: the sweep of Christ's entire career from pre-existent 'God' to triumphant and ascended Lord are all echoed in this ancient hymn. Yet no less remarkable is the concentration upon Christ's willing participation in the lot of humanity. The phrase 'he did not count equality with God a thing to be grasped' most likely refers to the temptation of Adam to be 'as God', which was at the heart of his fall. Adam, to put it another way, fell because of his unwillingness to accept the high role and honour he had been given — he wanted more; something higher and better. The true man, however, who alone had the right to claim equality because of his essential divinity, did not cling to his prerogatives and opportunities. Instead he showed his true humanity by willing acceptance of his incarnation. He partook of the human condition deliberately and willingly in order to restore to man his proper place near to God. His life of total dedication to God in obedient living found its highest expression of sacrifice in the humiliation of the cross. It goes almost without saying that Paul believed that the cross of Christ has objective significance — that is, it did something to save mankind. But in Philippians 2:5-11, as in Romans 5:12, the death of Jesus exemplifies the obedience of the last Adam who, as representative man, tastes death for all so that all may be partakers of a new humanity of which he is the Head.

Jesus as image

The term 'image' (*eikon*) when used of God, only occurs about twelve times in the New Testament and we could easily ignore its importance because of that fact. But as it occurs in some of the most significant passages in the Epistles we cannot brush it aside lightly.

We saw in Chapter 2 that in the Genesis account man is made in God's image but because of man's disobedience and wilful rejection of a relationship with the Creator this image is defaced in some way, with the corollary of loss of meaning and loss of identity. Man's essence is severed from his existence, we could say. In Paul's term he has 'fallen short of the glory of God'; that is, the growth-potential of his nature, dependent upon that relationship with God, has come to nothing.

Yet in Jesus the second Adam the 'image' idea now finds its true focus and, indeed, its full content. There are two main passages in Paul that it is necessary to consider. The first is Colossians 1:15 where Paul is setting out the superiority of Christ over all other claimants to the title of Lord. The nature of the heresy at Colossae has no bearing upon our study so we can leave that problem aside. In this passage, known as the 'Great Christology', Paul acclaims Jesus 'the image (*eikon*) of the invisible God, the first-born of all creation'. It is obvious from the context that the application of the word 'image' to Jesus describes a status and glory that is unique. He stands apart from the created order altogether. This is confirmed by the description of him as the 'first-born of all creation'. This is not to be taken as meaning that he is the first created being, as heretical groups since the Arians of the fourth century have argued. The idea of time does not enter into this; how could he be the eldest created being when his agency in creation implies his priority over it? No, it means that Christ is supreme over all things. This is indeed an amazing description of the man from Nazareth. So Professor C. F. D. Moule comments, 'the identification of that person — the Nazarene so ignominiously executed — with the subject of this description is staggering, and fairly cries out for some explanation.'[7] But no explicit explanation is given by Paul although a very adequate explanation is implicit in the passage, namely that through the work of Christ a new humanity is being created which transcends all that has gone before. Indeed, the repetition of the word 'firstborn' in v. 18, 'the firstborn from the dead' unites the two ideas of creation and redemption. Creator of all he becomes head of a new humanity through incarnation and resurrection.

There can be little doubt then that behind the meaning of this passage there lies the idea of the first and last Adams. Although as we noted above the 'image' idea stresses the divinity of Jesus, it finds its locus in the 'Adam' picture of Genesis 1:27. On the one hand Jesus is the 'image of the invisible God'. To the modern mind this is hardly a logical thing to say — after all, how is it possible to have an image of something intangible and without form? But it is our understanding of image that is getting in the way, not the word itself. In our thinking an image is a physical or symbolical representation of something else. But for Paul and his contemporaries the image did not stand apart from the thing signified but participated in it. There was an essential identity between 'image' and 'reality'. In this sense, then, Christ is the external manifestation of God himself. A similar idea is expressed in John 14:9: 'he who has seen me has seen the Father' or in Irenaeus's words, 'the Father had revealed Himself to all by making His Word visible to all.'[8] Yet, on the other hand, it is hard to resist seeing in the image-concept the thought that Christ is what Adam was intended to be. Jesus is the exact representation of what man was created to be — destined for sonship and glory.

The second passage which has already been discussed earlier but must now be considered again from a different point of view is Philippians 2:5-11. In this passage the word 'image' does not appear as such. The passage simply says of Christ that 'being in the form (*morphe*) of God he did not count equality with God a thing to be grasped' (v. 6). While the whole passage is still under close examination by scholars, it is generally believed that the Genesis story of the fall is the background of the hymn. The fact that the Greek word *morphe* (form) corresponds to and may translate the Hebrew word *zelem* (image) confirms that we should look to Genesis 1:26 to elucidate the meaning. So with O. Cullmann we argue that 'being in the form of God' is not merely a description of the divine nature of Jesus, but a statement about his stature as true man made in God's image.[9] This fits in better with the following verses which describe the outworking of the life of humility, service and obedience. In both of these great passages, therefore, Christ is seen as the true image of God and true man. He is what we could describe as 'paradigm' man in that he shows the possibilities of human existence when it is lived for God and with God.

With the notion of 'paradigm' man we pass to a second way in which the term 'image' is used in the New Testament, that is, to describe the new nature which all Christians share. Because Christ is the true likeness of God as well as Creator of the new humanity, we have in him alone the promise and power of the renewal of sinful man. But we need to note that although to be 'in Christ' is to belong to the 'new creation' (*kaine ktisis*, 2 Cor. 5:17), the work of the transformation is not instantaneous but gradual. Thus in Colossians 3:10 Paul contrasts the old nature, with its sinful ways, with 'the new nature which is being renewed in knowledge after the image of the creator'. It is not clear who is meant by 'creator' in that

verse, but as the context is speaking of Christ as the centre of
unity we assume that the reference is to him. The fact that
the only other reference to creator in Colossians (1:15) is to
Jesus would confirm this view.

But how does the transformation take place? Jesus himself
is the key to the process of transformation. So Paul says 'for
those whom he foreknew he also predestined to be con-
formed to the image of his son, that he might be the first born
among brethren' (Rom. 8:29). Conformity to the likeness of
Christ is not a kind of mystical contemplation of the Lord —
however helpful that can be — but to be Christ-like. Indeed,
in the context of Paul's words, it is a description of 'those who
love God'. In another passage Paul expresses the direction of
the Christian life in these words: 'that I may know him and
the power of his resurrection and may share his sufferings
becoming like him in his death' (Phil. 3:10). There is here a
curious reciprocal act in the relationship between Christ and
the believer. On the one hand Christ as man represents men
in his incarnation, death and resurrection. He tastes death for
all that all may live. Yet, on the other hand, his death and
resurrection are 'representative' acts in which his people have
to participate. The Christian cannot know life except by the
glad acceptance in his life that when Christ died, he also
died. (See Rom. 6:4ff; Col. 3:1). Just as Christ shared the
humiliation of man, so man through him is able to participate in Christ's glory. Yet, as Paul makes clear in Philippians
3 this comes about only through identification in Christ's
sufferings. So Paul significantly switches resurrection and
crucifixion around: 'That I may know him and the power of
his resurrection, and may share his sufferings, becoming like
him in his death.' It is only through the power of his
resurrection, in fact, that we can live like that. The image
expressed completely in Christ is gradually realised in us as
we become more like him.

The significance of Jesus

It is obvious that if Jesus were man only, however extraordinary and perfect, he could have little practical relevance
to future generations. He could serve as a good example,

perhaps, but there would be no compelling reason why his thoughts should mould present-day thinking. If only man, he would be simply akin to other outstanding people — a moral freak or a moral genius, depending on what attitude we take. But in Christian thought Jesus, although man, is more than man; the life he lived, the claims he made (as well as those made by his followers) together with the evidence of a filial consciousness with God, all point to an extraordinary dimension in his life. Christianity, indeed, since the New Testament and on the basis of it, has asserted that the paradox of Jesus is only solved by confessing him to be both God and man. It claims that Jesus is not merely a man who 'made it' by the perfection of his life (a heresy known as adoptionism); neither that he was 'God' who only appeared to be man (a heresy called docetism); but that 'God' and 'man' are both proper and meaningful terms to use of Jesus. The New Testament Church saw in him the disclosure of God as well as the manifestation of true man. Although we have been basing our arguments on the confession of the infant Church, the elements of this confession, that Jesus is the divine and reigning Lord, are clearly present in the life and work of Jesus who without overtly claiming to be God, acts like God and impressed his contemporaries with the uncanny 'likeness'. Such is the close and almost inextricable link between his perfect manhood and his divine sonship that the early Church could only explain his perfect 'humanity' in terms of divinity — that only 'God' could live like that.

But with such categories as 'humanity' and 'divinity' we face the essential mystery of the incarnation: how could Christ save us if he were not a human being like ourselves? Yet, how could a human being like ourselves save us? The New Testament leaves this dilemma unanswered — it was sufficient for the followers of Jesus to 'know' that he belonged to mankind and yet belonged to God. This creed they proclaimed confidently, fully recognising its logical inconsistency but believing that it answered the facts theologically. They assumed, indeed, that only God could be Saviour and that only by his participation in mankind could humanity be restored to God once again.

We started this chapter with two questions: 'why single out

Jesus from among great men?' and 'did he achieve anything of lasting importance that affects all mankind?' The Christian replies that the universal and timeless significance of Jesus boils down to two crucial elements. Firstly, Jesus does the work of God in coming among men to redeem them, forgive them and restore them to the family of God. He represents God. Secondly, he reveals human nature not only as it is, weak and in need of God, but as it should be — fully human. He is, in Luther's famous phrase, the 'proper man'; man as he is really designed to be. He represents man. These two bases form the theological framework for his significance. But we have to look elsewhere for the practical relevance of Jesus, the man from Nazareth. Where is this to be found? Surely in only one place, the only place indeed where Jesus would wish it to be found, that is in his ability to meet the eternal needs of men. John Robinson, in his book *The Human Face of God*, narrates how on a poster stating that 'Christ is the answer' someone had written beneath 'yes, but to what question?'. It may be true that Christians have claimed too much for Christ with the net effect that his real mission has been obscured. Christ does not answer all our questions, neither is he the remedy to all our problems. But he does answer man's most basic question: 'how may I become a whole person?' Made whole, of course, we can answer the other questions in his power and by his guidance. Only Jesus, the Christian believes, can remove the barrier between God and man and remake man as he was meant to be. A. M. Allchin once wrote, 'In Christ we read the riddle of our origins.'[10] This is principally because Jesus speaks inexhaustibly to the deepest needs of men, becoming a focus for hope and a symbol of identity because of his oneness with us. But what about his rivals today? We can name innumerable secular as well as religious figures whom people identify with and make exclusive claims for. How is it possible to know which is true? There are no easy answers to this, neither have there ever been, for ever since the birth of Christianity Christ has had his rivals for the heart of man. One answer is to compare the nature of the leaders of the respective movements and to study their different systems of belief. In this respect the Christian will say on the basis of fact that Christ is incomparable.

But another answer lies in experience. Jesus becomes our Lord, in the expression of John Robinson, 'as we find and affirm his unique ability to shape our lives.'[11] If Christ does not have relevance for daily living then his mission has failed and his claims are false. Christians might as well shut up shop and go home; all they have left is an elaborate web of self-deception. But, as Christian history shows, it is in experience that Christ's relevance finds its vindication. Not that Christians are perfect! Far from it. Christian history reveals many sobering examples of failure, sin, and evil all enacted in the name of Christ. But the constant miracle of changed lives, modelled on the pattern of Jesus's humanity and lived in his power, continues to this day. Every conversion proclaims that Jesus is Lord.

NOTES

1 S. Kierkegaard, *The Concept of Dread* (Princeton University Press, 1957), p. 82.
2 *The Mediator* (Lutterworth, 1934), p. 364.
3 *Sunday Times*, Nov. 18th, 1973.
4 R. Niebuhr, *The Nature and Destiny of Man*, II, p. 57.
5 *Adversus haereses*, V. 21.
6 *Adv. haer.*, II.22.4.
7 C. F. D. Moule, *Commentary on Colossians* (Cambridge Greek Series), p. 59.
8 *Adv. haer.*, IV. 6.5.
9 O. Cullmann, *The Christology of the New Testament* (SCM, 1963), p. 176.
10 *Man: Fallen and Free*, ed. E. W. Kemp (Hodder and Stoughton, 1969), ch. 7.
11 *The Human Face of God* (SCM, 1973), p. 238.

CHAPTER 5

Christian Existence

CHRISTIANITY IS SUMMED up in one word — Christ. In his incarnation, crucifixion and resurrection God becomes fully involved with the destiny of man. In his *incarnation* we find the model for our humanity; in his *crucifixion* man's utter sinfulness is symbolised in the cross as he becomes 'sin for us'; and in his *resurrection* there is new hope for mankind as he is raised from the grave. In these three integrated 'moments' we have not only the heart of the Christian faith but also the starting point for the Christian life. Significantly, the New Testament writers rarely use the human life of Jesus alone as the key for Christian life and behaviour. Perhaps the reason is that, though his life is the example of true human existence, the quality of that life mocks man's inability to rise to such a lofty standard. Mercifully, the New Testament idea of the Christian life is based very firmly on these three elements of incarnation, crucifixion and resurrection. The gospel of Christ does not merely say, 'Live like me and you will be saved' but 'You cannot be saved unless you die and my life lives within you.'

We often fail to realise how revolutionary this gospel really is. Our familiarity with it, surrounded as we are by the trappings and traditions of established religion, may have rendered innocuous its challenge to man's self-respect and self-esteem. Have we, indeed, made respectable and commonplace a most startling and outrageous attack on the nature of man? It was certainly seen as both in the first century. Startling, because the declaration that only God can make men whole is an all-out attack on both the haughty pride of the Jew in his 'righteousness' and the egotistic confidence of the Greek in his 'wisdom'. Outrageous, because it totally abrogates the value man puts upon himself. It denies his essential goodness or his capacity to save himself. Yet the 'good news' of this apparently pessimistic message had astonishing success in the period of the New Testament. Thousands, like Paul, found their deepest longings satisfied in Christianity; they found also the power to live victoriously. Millions of Christians since have testified to the same experience, and it continues to be the experience of people today as they turn to Christ, that in him and through him the truly authentic life may be lived.

What is this Christian existence? This may appear a somewhat naïve question. Not only is it a greatly explored issue but nearly two thousand years of Christian history should have given us a few clues by now! True; but in every new generation it is still necessary to pose the question. Confusion reigns about what it means to live a genuine Christian life in the modern world. Claims and counter-claims are made about the Christian life which seem to have a very precarious connection with New Testament teaching. There is for example, the '*triumphalist*' interpretation which says: 'Come to Christ and all your problems will be solved. You can have happiness now, and complete healing to your body and mind. God can meet all your needs.' To parody a credit-system advertisement, this type of Christianity takes 'the waiting out of wanting'. Such a 'have it all now' approach fails to appreciate the dynamic quality of salvation which is never fulfilled or completed in this life. The triumphalist approach confuses earth and heaven. An equally false interpretation, the complete opposite of the one just mentioned, is one we may call the '*dour*' approach; it is often associated with radical or liberal forms of Christianity. It says, 'We can promise you no certainty and little joy in your Christian experience; we can expect only sweat and tears, as we try to work out our Christian faith in the world.' We salute such a brave Christianity: it seems to accord, after all, with the rugged spirit of Jesus as he approached his death in Jerusalem. But such a dour Christian existence finds few echoes in the New Testament taken as a whole: Jesus, after all, did offer life, joy, peace and power to his followers. There is, thirdly an interpretation which David Moberg calls the *Comfort Camp*,[1] but which I prefer to describe as '*milk and water*' Christianity. Instead of saying with Christ, 'Come, take up the cross and follow me', it makes Christ say, 'Come lie on my cushion; rest in an interpretation of life that will give you peace and shield you from life's storms; have peace without too heavy a price, and a faith without too many demands.' This third approach, the pietistic quietism so typical of Western Christianity, is probably the most serious distortion of the three because it makes it seem as if Christ calls people to an easy, problem-free existence.

All three approaches caricature various modern attempts to live the Christian life, but they are sufficiently close to reality to make the question, 'What *is* the authentic Christian life?' relevant and urgent. Can we produce from the New Testament a picture of the genuine Christian life that might be a model for the Christian today? To be a Christian — is it to be more human, less human or even sub-human? If modern man were able to see the Christian life clearly, would he find it in any sense a desirable option?

A BIBLICAL PORTRAIT OF THE CHRISTIAN

Death and Life

The New Testament makes it clear that the Christian life pivots on the life, death and resurrection of Jesus. Paul ties together the death and resurrection of the Lord with the existence of the Christian, 'we are convinced that one died for all; therefore all died. And he died for all that those who live might no longer live for themselves but for him who for their sake died and was raised' (2 Cor. 5:14, 15). The Christian life begins with death as a man turns away from himself to follow Christ. Bonhoeffer expressed it memorably: 'When Christ calls a man he bids him come and die.'[2] But what kind of death is this? The New Testament replies that there must be a realisation of our deep need for God, a need which transcends mere head-knowledge of our unworthiness and penetrates our inner being. No-one can come into a proper relationship with God until, like Paul in despair (Rom. 7), he comes face to face with his moral bankruptcy. So Jesus declared pointedly to the Pharisees who objected at his friendship with 'sinners' that he had come 'not to call the righteous but sinners to repentance.' Jesus is always surrounded by people who are sinners and know it.

What about those who have come into Christianity through other gateways — through the need for friendship, or because of love and admiration of Christ, or because of the life of the Church? We may have friends who have entered not because of any obvious crying need, but because they identify with the Christian faith and find themselves more complete by being part of the Church. Are these things valueless? Indeed not; but it must be stressed firmly that unless there is an awareness of our spiritual need and sinful plight we can know the gospel only in part. Any form of Christianity which does not have a theology of man's spiritual bankruptcy is seriously defective. There can be no question about it; the realisation of one's own liability to save oneself — a death experience if ever there was one — becomes God's moment of salvation and the commencement of life. The word used in the New Testament to denote this decisive action is the verb 'to repent', which actually means 'to change one's mind' or 'to change the direction of one's life'. There are negative and positive sides to this. Negatively, it means to turn *away* from former goals and gods; positively, it describes a turning *to* God, recognising that his claims can be denied no longer. Robert Penn Warren showed profound understanding of this process in his poem *Brother to Dragons* even though he was not attempting to describe the experience of Christian conversion. His words, placed on the lips of his character Thomas Jefferson, describe the moment of 'healing' for a man:

The recognition of complicity is the beginning of innocence.
The recognition of necessity is the beginning of freedom.
The recognition of the direction of fulfilment is the death of self.
And the death of the self is the beginning of selfhood.

Grace and faith

Once man has repented, once he has said 'yes' to God —
God takes the initiative in his life; he steps in and takes over.
The basis of this almost incredible act of redeeming worthless
man is described in the New Testament by the word 'grace'
(*charis*). 'By grace you have been saved through faith, and this
is not your own doing, it is the gift of God, not of works, lest
any man should boast' (Eph. 2:8,9). Grace is the unmerited
love of God as he intervenes in the mess that man has made of
himself and his world. 'God's loving action in Christ' is
perhaps a more accurate definition because Christ's life for
others is an embodiment of God's grace. 'We beheld his
glory,' John's Gospel announces, 'full of grace and truth'
(1:14). God's act of saving mankind through the ministry of
Christ is an act of sheer undeserved generosity. It is the act of
love which welcomes home gladly and freely the prodigal son.
No reason can be produced for such a surprising act — only a
relationship between God and man far beyond man's understanding explains it.

If grace is the basis of man's new life in Christ, faith is
surely the means of appropriating it. 'You have been saved
through faith,' declares Ephesians 2:8. Such faith is not
merely a form of belief that 'hopes for the best' but the
committed trust of a man who has come to the end of his own
resources; a wholehearted trust in the faithfulness of God.
Martin Luther saw very clearly this connection between faith
and possession; in his phrase 'he who believes has' he captures
the operation and the content of faith. It is not only the
gateway to life but also the means of inheriting the promises
of God.

Grace and faith; these two great words are at the heart of
New Testament Christianity. All that mankind can proffer
are empty hands to receive the gift of God. *Sola gratia, sola fide*
— by grace alone, through faith alone; there is no other way.

A Christian, then, is a person to whom something remarkable has happened. Realising his need he has turned to the
living God in repentance and faith, and is declared not only
forgiven but also a child of God. In all this, inevitably, we are

faced by elements beyond our comprehension. It is not immediately obvious to us why we should be accepted by God, neither is it clear why Christ's act of self-giving sacrifice should have such effect. How do we know that it is not, after all, a gigantic hoax? An implausible mythology which only fools the gullible? The proof of the pudding is in the eating; and it is in human living that the truth of Christianity is confirmed.

Confirmation 1 — the witness of the new life

Paul declares, 'If any man be in Christ he is a new creation' (*kaine ktisis*, 2 Cor. 5:17). The phrase 'in Christ' is one of Paul's favourite terms for the new life, describing the deep, permanent and joyful relationship between the new Christian and his Lord; a life which can only be thought of in terms of a totally different form of existence. In the writings of John, the radical nature of this encounter with Christ is envisaged in a similar way, as a 'new birth' and as being 'born again'.

But what is the character of this event which can only be considered in terms of newness of life and separation from the old? The New Testament answers this in terms of the change which takes place in the personality of the new convert. His goals are different; he has an overwhelming love for Christ and a desire to serve him. His attitudes are different; he possesses a love for others and joy and satisfaction in life. His daily living is different; he is given the strength through Christ to live the Christian life. If sin is, as John Oman once said, 'the attempt to get out of life what God has not put into it',[3] we may view this new existence in Christ as the fulfilment of life, as God puts back what should have been there in the first place.

Significantly, however, this new life is never separated from the family of God of which the new believer is now a member. For Paul, to be 'in Christ' is the same as being 'in the Church' because it is to be part of the redeemed. community of Jesus Christ. The unequivocal teaching of the New Testament — that there can be no Christianity without the Church — is registered in Paul's teaching concerning baptism, which is treated not only as the entrance into the

Christian body but also as an expression of the new life in God (Rom. 6:1; Eph. 1:13). The two are inseparable because no one can live the Christian life alone. The new Christian, of course, needs the nurture of the Christian family if he is to mature into discipleship, and the community needs the enthusiasm and insights of the new believer to maintain the freshness and relevance of its own life. Furthermore, the Christian family will be the place, as all families are, where the joys of love are experienced by the new member (1 Thess. 1:3) and where mistakes are greeted by love and acceptance (Eph. 4:25-32).

Confirmation 2 — the witness of the Spirit

Obviously we cannot and should not separate the Spirit from the new life offered in Christ. The Spirit, after all, is the 'Spirit of life in Christ Jesus' (Rom. 8:2) and he is at the heart of any turning to God. But the Spirit's activity is not confined to the new birth. Growth, as well as the gift of life belongs to his function; he indwells the Christian to make him more like his Lord, and he opens to him the richness and abundance of relationship with Almighty God. Two important words are used in the New Testament of the Christian's possession of the Spirit. The first word is 'aparche' which is usually translated 'first-fruits' (Rom. 8:23). This word would have been familiar to a Jew of the first century because it signified the first harvest sheaf offered to God. As well as being a tangible sign of the harvest, it was also a pledge and promise on God's part of the fullness of the harvest still to come. The second word arrabon was a well-known commercial term in the first century. It was the down-payment given by a purchaser when a bargain was made. As well as being a first instalment, it was also a promise and guarantee that the rest of the money would follow in due course. We are familiar with the idea, if not the term, from hire-purchase agreements today. So Ephesians 1:13,14 speaks of the Spirit as being the 'guarantee (arrabon) of our inheritance until we acquire possession of it' (see also 2 Cor. 1:22; 5:5). The striking thing about both words, in spite of their different backgrounds, is that they signify something that is tangibly given to the Christian;

namely the Spirit himself. He is the *first-fruit* and he is the *first instalment*. While both words have an unmistakable future reference they show just as clearly that there is a definite present reality. There should not be any doubt in the Christian's experience concerning the gift he has been given. 'But,' says someone, 'what tangible evidence can you direct me to look to in my life for reassurance that I have the Spirit?' The Biblical answer is that the Spirit leaves his unmistakable hallmark not usually in rapturous feelings or ecstatic experiences but in more common-place things. For example; the desire to know more of God and Christ, the hunger for the Word of God, a willingness to serve Christ in the world, a love for Christian fellowship — in ways like these we have tangible signs of the Spirit's presence.

Confirmation 3 — by-products

We may describe the two elements mentioned above, the new life in Christ and the indwelling presence of the Holy Spirit, as the main constituents of the Christian life. But the results are important too. Let us consider just four of the by-products of this new relationship with God; peace, access, freedom and joy. The Hebrew word for peace, *shalom* was very rich in its associations for Jewish people. Its basic root meant 'well-being' and described the wholeness of man, both in physical health and the spiritual relationship to God. In fact, *shalom* conveyed much the same meaning as the word salvation. The Jew looked forward longingly to the establishment of God's *shalom* because it expressed God's dwelling with men, and he could not wish a greater blessing on anyone than that of *shalom*. It is not by accident that the Risen Christ came among his disciples with the words 'peace be with you'. In John 20 this phrase occurs three times, indicating that John saw the significance of Christ's work in the entrance of God's *shalom* in the world. Now through the Risen Christ there is the opportunity for man to grow up into the wholeness of relationship with God (see also Eph. 2:14-17; Rom. 14:17; Rom. 15:17; John 14:27). Now through the work of Christ the barrier of sin is destroyed and the justified person has 'peace with God through our Lord Jesus Christ'

(Rom. 5:1). But 'peace' is also used in another sense in the
New Testament to describe calmness, tranquillity and confidence in God in the midst of darkness and in the centre of
stress. It is from a prison, no less, that Paul writes to a small
congregation that 'the peace of God which passes all understanding will keep (literally 'garrison') your hearts and minds
in Christ Jesus' (Phil. 4:7). Here is a promise that those who
have experienced that reconciling peace of God may have
daily peace in the context of daily living.

'Access' to God is another by-product of being a Christian.
Like *shalom* it is another rich and significant word. Its
background is that of the court of an oriental king. The Greek
playwright Xenophon tells that in the court of the Persian
king there was an official called the 'introducer' (the Greek
word is *prosagogeus* which comes from the same root as
'access') and his function was to introduce people into the
royal presence. Inevitably such an introduction was eagerly
sought after, but rarely granted. Few ordinary people ever
saw the face of the king; that was the privilege of the rich and
noble. This background illuminates the work that Jesus does
for men. Through him man is brought into the royal presence
of God, not just for a fleeting few minutes but with freedom
to enter his courts without fear, confident that the access is
eternal. And, what is more, access to this King is open to all
people — poor, as well as rich. The word also sheds light on
the role of prayer (cf. 1 Tim. 2:1; Rom. 8:26). The Christian
prays not because it is a religious duty, but because he knows
that God is his heavenly Father who hears him and who longs
for a close, ever-deepening, relationship with his children.
The breaking down of the barriers between God and man
means that nothing on God's side will ever stop the prayer-
relationship that man is encouraged to build up.

A third result of the presence of God within the believer is
'freedom'. Before a person becomes a Christian, declares the
New Testament, he is in bondage to his desire, unable to
break away from the shackles of the past or the presence of sin
now. As we saw in Chapter 3 Paul summarises brilliantly the
predicament of man in his letter to the Romans. He describes
man's condition as being a 'slave' to sin and helpless in the
face of sin's great allure and power (Rom. 6:7; 5:15). What is

more, conscience and the Law confronted him as sentinels, accusing him of wrongdoing, mocking his claim for freedom and responsibility. But now in Christ, Paul says, speaking from his own experience, the believer is free from the bondage and power of sin because he serves not under the old written code but in the new life of the Spirit (Rom. 7:6). Freedom to do anything, then? No, certainly not, but we do have real freedom, freedom to be 'human' before God and to employ that freedom in responsible moral ways that typify the really free man. Paul, in fact, claims that true freedom emerges from a new form of slavery — that is, slavery to God. But, mark you, it is a 'slavery' chosen willingly and gladly because of the full recognition now that the individual cannot live the Christian life by himself but only in God's strength.

Finally, we single out 'joy' as another and important ingredient in the Christian life. It is a present reality as the deep peace of God is experienced, as sins are forgiven, and as the Christian is made whole. The tag that Christianity is 'pie in the sky when you die' is a travesty of the truth, The fact is that the Christian hope is vindicated in the here and now. But possessing Christ's joy is not to be interpreted as living in an unreal world of ecstasy or a state of euphoria. It is the overflow of the experience of God's presence in our daily situation. Paul himself describes Christian joy in his letter to the Philippians. For him the Christian faith was no arid, academic thing, but an ever present experience of the reality of his Lord. Paul never got over the wonder of salvation. Hence his encouragement to 'rejoice in the Lord and again, I say, rejoice' (Phil. 4:4). Why? Because the Lord is at hand (v. 5), because he answers prayer (v. 6), because he gives peace (v. 7), because he gives strength (v. 13), because he gives contentment (v. 13) and because he can meet our deepest needs (v. 19). Is joy, then, to be viewed as the automatic possession of Christians? We know only too well that this is not the case. There are times when despair and unhappiness invade our hearts and minds. Paul's use of the imperative *'rejoice* in the Lord, and again I say rejoice', indicates that joy is to be fought for, and is expected to come as our hearts and minds become open to the presence and peace of God. But joy contains also the expectation of good things to come. So

Romans 5:2 can say, 'We rejoice in hope of sharing the glory
of God.' In other words, meaning has been found for the
future as well as for today. Christian joy, therefore, is twofold:
we rejoice in Christ now and all that he has done, but we look
ahead joyfully and expectantly to the day when that joy will
be complete at the sight of our living Lord.

THE GOAL OF THE CHRISTIAN LIFE

Although the Christian is 'in Christ' the goal of this new
relationship is summed up in the phrase 'putting on Christ'
(Rom. 13:14) by which is meant the living out of this
relationship day by day, and thereby growing like Christ
himself. We need to be clear about this; at no point in his
Christian life and experience can he say 'I have arrived'.
Although he is part of the family of God and therefore secure
in that relationship he is called to live as a son and heir. A
'new creation' he may be, but this does not mean that he is
perfect and sinless — indeed, experience will soon shatter
such complacency. The thrust of Paul's argument is that we
are called to be what we already are; to let the inner reality of
our relationship with Christ manifest itself in our conduct.
Although a new creation in Christ, the individual is still
subject to the old nature and its demands and this involves
him in a daily battle. He is, as the Reformation thinkers
realised *simul justus et peccator*, both just and sinful: *justus*
because of the merits of Christ and *peccator* by reason of his
human nature. At no stage during his earthly life will he be
able to claim complete holiness or perfection. A child of
heaven he may be, but while he is bound to this existence he
is caught between the call of the new life to be holy and the
temptations of world, flesh and the devil which lure him
along a different road.

This call to 'put on Christ' or to 'be holy' is commonly
known as 'sanctification' by which is meant the ongoing
transformation of human life towards the model of Christ. It
is instructive to note how in Paul's letters the demand for
action follows the statement of a theological truth; so in
Colossians 3:1 'if you have been raised with Christ seek those
things that are above...put to death, therefore, what is earthly

in you'. Clearly Paul had no use for a religious experience which did not translate itself into action, and he would certainly agree that a justification cannot be real if it does not issue in growth. 'Babes' in Christ must become mature Christians (Eph. 4:14; Heb. 6:6; Col. 3:1); the old nature must be put off and the new life lived in Christ's power (Eph. 4:22,24). The growth that is expected is that of growth in holiness and knowledge, that is, in behaviour and spiritual insight. On the one hand, the individual is reminded that 'his body is the temple of the Holy Spirit' and purity should govern all his relationships, and, on the other hand, he is called to grow in knowledge of God's will and of the love of Christ (Eph. 3:19; Col. 2:2,3). This, of course, is a most daunting challenge and it is little wonder that even Paul confesses that he was far short of completion — 'not as though I had already attained,' he exclaims, 'or were already made mature, but I press on to make it my own, because Christ Jesus has made me his own' (Phil. 3:12).

The Christian life, then, is a form of creative tension between 'already' and 'not yet'. The Christian is saved, knows Christ, is indwelt by the Spirit and possesses God's peace, freedom and joy, but in none of these areas is he complete. In fact, he is compelled to press on and grow because he cannot stand still in the Christian life. Part of this growth involves the recognition of, and response to a number of important tensions which are part of human Christian experience. Let us consider two areas that are centres of discussion and controversy.

1. The tension between the flesh and spirit

We have already denied the suggestion that sinlessness is possible during the earthly life of man, yet this mistaken view monotonously and destructively emerges from time to time in Christian history.

The basis for this so-called 'perfectionism' is the assumption that the New Testament teaches that the Christian is released completely from the power of sin and is now able to walk in newness of life. After all, didn't Paul say that 'he who has died is free from sin' (Rom. 6:7)? And isn't this idea affirmed in the Epistle of John: 'no one who abides in him sins; no one who sins has either seen him or knows him' (1 John 3:6)? The early Church, furthermore, not only assumed that perfection was possible but was commanded by the gospel. The entire penitential system of merits and making satisfaction for post-baptismal sin is, in fact, founded upon this idea. But perfectionism must face two formidable and fundamental questions: Is it theologically correct, and is it consonant with human experience?

Let us first of all challenge the idea that Paul himself was a champion of sinlessness in Christian experience. He does, indeed, say three times in Romans 6:1-11 that the Christian has died to sin (vv. 2, 7, 11). But does this really indicate that sin has no more effect upon the individual, and that he is liberated from its power and influence once and for all? It all depends upon what is meant by a 'death unto sin'. Those who urge some form of sinlessness usually take this phrase to indicate that the nature of the Christian is so changed that he is beyond the power of sin and can now do God's will completely. The context, however, flatly refutes this suggestion. The most obvious interpretation is that the Christian through baptism is identified with the death of Christ in his victory over the penalty and power of sin. The redeemed person is dead to sin in the sense that through Christ he shares in that victory and now lives the new life. He has passed out of the sphere of the bondage of sin into a new Kingdom. But the Christian in this world is not simply a new being; he continues to exhibit the 'old' nature as well. Paul clearly recognised that sin is a possibility in the life of the believer, otherwise he would not have warned his readers that sin must not reign in their mortal bodies (Rom. 6:12), neither must they yield their 'members to sin as instruments of wickedness' (v. 13). To be 'free from sin' (v. 18) which is part of the promise of the gospel, is not the same as to be sinless, and this, in fact, is the basic confusion. Through Christ the Christian is free, but Paul knew, as each of us knows, that while Christ offers power over sin, the Christian lives in a world darkened by its presence. He lives, in fact, in two environments, in Christ and in the world, and woe betide him if he underestimates the power of either Christ or sin. He is free from the penalty of sin and is a new creature in Christ, but he cannot escape the influence of sin or avoid being caught up in its effects in the world. To be human is to be part of a sinful world, whether we are redeemed or not.

Thus to claim sinlessness, or complete freedom from sin in any form, or to claim that the Christian's old nature is now unresponsive to sin, is nonsense. Whoever heard of a combatant on the front line of battle asserting that he is free from danger in any shape or form? But, to continue this analogy, the Christian is always on the battle-front, and the post he mans is exposed continually to the attack of evil. Once he was a prisoner in enemy-held territory; now, on the one hand, he is 'free from sin', but, on the other, by no means free from its temptations or effects. He is now on God's side of the battle to be sure, but there is a complicating factor (and this is where the analogy breaks down); not only is the Christian on the 'frontier' but he is the frontier! Not only is the battle going on in the world but it goes on in the Christian! So here is a fundamental and profound paradox. On the one hand we are free and no longer slaves; if this were not so why would we be encouraged to fight against sin if we had no strength in Christ to do so? On the other hand, there is no room for complacency, or for a theory of sinfulness which sets up the Christian like a benign Buddha gazing down indifferently on the pressures and effects of evil. The warnings throughout the New Testament concerning the need for watchfulness show perfectionism as a false idealisation of the Christian life. It is not only false, it is dangerous. Much distress can be caused to sensitive individuals by insisting that they must be 'pockets' of perfect holiness in this sinful world in order to qualify as Christians. The inevitable clash between such a demand and their own experience robs them of all the assurance the Lord wants them to enjoy.

The tension we have been describing is, according to Paul, a tension between flesh and spirit: the flesh which shares in the fallenness of the world, and the spirit which is the sphere of God's presence (Rom. 8:1-11).

The fact of this tension calls, not for arrogance, but for *humility*. 'Let him who thinks he stands take heed lest he fall,' warns Paul in 1 Corinthians 10:12. The power of sin is greater when we claim to have conquered it completely. C. H. Spurgeon drily but accurately observed on the claim of perfection by another Christian, 'We all thought our brother was perfect until he told us so!'

It also calls for *vigilance* and common sense. 'Know thyself' is not only Socratic wisdom, it is Christian common sense as well. Because we are weak it is foolhardy to place ourselves in positions of temptation however strong we may consider ourselves to be. Shakespeare expresses the danger concisely: In *The Tempest* Prospero refers to Ferdinand's vow to honour his beloved Miranda, 'Look thou be true; do not give dalliance too much the rein — the strongest oaths are straw to the fire in the blood; be more abstemious or else, good night your vow!' (Act IV, Sc. I).

It calls, thirdly for God's *power* to overcome sin and temptation. The Christian may not be sinless but in Christ he is free because Christ has conquered the power of sin, evil and death. So the Lord claims, 'If the Son make you free you will be free indeed' (John 8:36). Christians need not be timid in testing this in daily experience. Are 'defeated' Christians today accepting too readily the triumph of evil?

Finally, this tension between flesh and spirit calls for *realism*. 'We wrestle not against flesh and blood,' says Ephesians 6:12, 'but against the spiritual hosts of wickedness in the heavenly places.' Yet God has sent into battle weak creatures of flesh and blood — so vulnerable and apparently defenceless. It would be foolish to retreat into starry-eyed idealism about such a conflict, or to be triumphalist concerning the outcome. Realism dictates that sinlessness is not a condition to apply to this world, but to the next, when the battle is done. It is in our daily life, our everyday existence, that sin makes its attack and it is here that it must be resisted. Here is the arena of our greatest victories and, sadly, our most ignominious defeats.

2. The tension between freedom and obedience

We normally associate freedom with its opposite — slavery. In one way this is correct because the Christian knows he has been freed from sin and death (Rom. 8:2), bondage (Rom.

6:18), guilt (Rom. 7:25) and wrath (Rom. 5:9). The New Testament makes it quite plain, however, that the individual is not free to do anything he wants because genuine freedom is only known in responsible obedience to God himself. Here is another fundamental paradox. Freedom to do anything ends up as freedom to do nothing because it is basically a call for anarchy. In Robbie Burns' poem *The Song of the Jolly Beggars* freedom and anarchy are confused:

> A fig for those by law protected,
> Liberty's a glorious feast,
> Courts for cowards were erected
> Churches built to please the priests.

Liberty must, in fact, have controls; otherwise anarchy inevitably results, leading to a different form of bondage possibly no less tyrannical than the one that preceded it. For example, when in May 1974 the Portuguese Army replaced fascism with democracy, within a matter of just a few weeks democracy itself was threatened by the popular demand for the immediate recognition of full rights and complete equality in matters of wages, living conditions, and social privileges. One commentator on the scene observed, 'The Portuguese were forgetting one simple fact familiar to those from advanced democratic countries, that freedom for me means freedom for you and everyone else, and unless this is remembered in responsible conduct freedom will soon degenerate into complete anarchy with no means of deciding the respective merits of the competing claims.'

Freedom for the Christian involves the constraint of service. 'Having been set free from sin,' says Paul, 'you have become slaves of righteousness' (Rom. 6:18). But this is not another grinding bondage but instead the willing agreement of former 'slaves', now 'sons', to serve, not under a legalistic code of 'dos' and 'dont's' but in the new life of the Spirit (Rom. 7:6). The Christian then exercises his freedom in obedience to the claims of God. The pattern for this is, of course, that of Christ himself. He is pictured in the New Testament as one who is both free and obedient. As the 'free one' his mission is his own glad and voluntary choice, and as

the 'obedient one' he does his Father's will in glad com-
pliance. The theme of obedience is one of the major strands
in the Gospel of John: 'I always do what is pleasing to him', is
Christ's claim (John 8:29; 7:16; 5:19).

In Christian experience the two concepts must be held
together in tension and not allowed to drift apart. As Dietrich
Bonhoeffer comments, 'Obedience without freedom is
slavery; freedom without obedience is arbitrary freewill.'[4] Yet
the combination of the two is a mark of genuine maturity.
Obedience on its own is blind and may lead to terrible deeds
as the history of Nazism shows. But the Christian is not
allowed the luxury of merely obeying blindly, whether the
voice he is listening to is the voice of the Church, the voice of
the Bible, or even what he believes is the voice of God. The
function of Christian freedom implies that everything is
subservient to the mind of Christ; but the Christian must not
duck the call to act as a responsible free person, although
guided by the Spirit working through the Church, Bible and
other means. On the other hand, freedom on its own is also
highly dangerous because like a pilotless vessel the Christian
can easily wander off course if there are no consistent 'rules' of
guidance to apply. Paul, we recall, attacked the boast of some
Christians at Corinth that through Christ they were free from
petty restrictions and could now live as liberated men.
Turning their cry of 'all things are lawful' against them, he
retorts, 'All things are lawful but not all things are helpful, all
things are lawful but not all things build up. Let no one seek
his own good but the good of his neighbour' (1 Cor. 10:24).
Here is the heart of true Christian freedom — it is never
egocentric but centred on the good of others, and its sphere
of activity is always in the area of responsibility towards
others.

As a result of this tension between freedom and obedience two critical problems emerge which bother Christians
from time to time. First of all, there is the question of the
law — to what extent are Christians free from its influence?
Secondly, there is the danger that should the constraint
of the law be removed, new forms of legalism might replace
it.

Are Christians free from the Law?

First impressions suggest that Paul gives a minimal place to the law in the Christian life. Indeed, he likens the Mosaic law to a *paidagogos*, that is, a slave whose duty it was to take the children of well-to-do parents to school. Once the children are grown up the slave's job is done. He says 'now that faith has come we are no longer under a *paidagogos*' (Gal. 3:24). We can easily get the wrong impression from Paul's comments. It almost seems as though the Law of Moses is abrogated by Christ and is no longer binding on those under the new Covenant; instead it is replaced by a more nebulous, 'airy-fairy', law of Christ.

This polarisation has been brought about by a confusion between the role of the law as a *way* of salvation and the law as a *guide* to the holiness God requires from man. As a system of salvation, which the Jews believed the Law to be, it is in Paul's opinion both accuser and failure; 'accuser' in that it mocks man's vain attempts to achieve a righteousness by merit, and 'failure' because of its impotence to save. Now, Paul meets the 'accusation' of the Law by stating that when Christ died the believer also 'died' to the Law (cf. Romans 6:11 and 7:4). That is, when a man is in Christ the Law no longer stands over against him as judge because Christ has met for all sinners the 'curse' of the Law, absorbing its condemnation on their behalf (Gal. 3:13). But this does not mean that the Law itself is now a dead letter as far as Christians are concerned. Far from it; its role has not disappeared — it has merely changed. Although Paul repudiates the idea that the Law constitutes the way to God, he does not cast it away altogether. It is still 'holy', 'good' and 'spiritual', bringing to light the real nature of sin (Rom. 7:7, 12, 13). Its judgmental functions cease when a person becomes a Christian and it is now a guide for life. Christ is, therefore, the 'end' of the Law (Rom. 10:4) in a twofold sense. First of all he has fulfilled its demands on behalf of all men. Secondly, he radically re-interprets it in the light of the claim of love. In so doing he attacked contemporary treatment of the Law which stressed its absolute and unconditional character. In Jesus's opinion no system, however good, should have such a stranglehold on people. Instead, he re-affirms the original framework of the Law which was the election and promise to the people of God. Christ, by his example in teaching and living, steers men back to viewing the Law not as constituting the wrath of God but his compassion and care for his people.

Therefore, when Paul speaks about the 'law of Christ' (Gal. 6:2) it is hardly likely that he was advocating the replacement of the Mosaic Law by love on its own. Love, in fact, does not annul Law but fulfils it. 'Owe no one anything,' writes Paul, 'except to love one another; for he who loves his neighbour has fulfilled the Law' (Rom. 14.8).

We are led to say, then, that all men — redeemed or otherwise — are under the Ten Commandments — the Law of God — which stands eternally and firmly as pointing to the standard of life to which God expects us to conform. But on their own, interpreted apart from the love of God, they can so easily become sterile, forbidding monuments of law, tyrannising and even debasing men. The Christian, however, sees in them God's gracious provision for the well-being of his people; and through the Spirit of God he is given the power, not only to 'delight in the Law' (Rom. 7:22) but progressively to keep it because he has been set free (Rom. 8:22). He obeys it, however, not to be forgiven, but because he has been forgiven.

Danger of a new legalism?

The second area relevant to modern Christians is the outworking of freedom in Christian living. Through Christ the individual is released from the bondage of Law and now dwells in the new world of grace. Are there governing principles that control and shape the new life in Christ? History has shown how new legal systems, no less savage and demanding, can take the place of the old law though called by kindlier names. The post-Reformation period shows, for example, how an arid Biblicism may replace an equally arid authoritarian structure in the Roman Church. In making the criticism we are not, of course, attacking the Bible but the misuse of it. The Bible must not be identified with God; it is the word of God to men in all ages and has to be interpreted wisely, carefully and in accord with the only key to Scripture — that is, Christ the Word. Lord Soper once remarked, 'The Bible is a marvellous servant but an intolerable master.' It becomes an intolerable master when it is misused and misinterpreted to bolster up the claims and codes of Christian groups who appeal to it for support, saying. 'To be a true Christian you must live as we live, follow our pattern of behaviour and our social customs, and live according to our systems of morality.' The attraction of such forms of Christian legalism lies in the framework of security they give people. The human spirit somehow loathes uncertainty or risk; it finds comfort when told clearly and authoritatively 'this is what you must do' or 'this is how the Christian life ought to be lived.'

Unfortunately for those who take refuge in such havens of religious security, whether it is by appeal to the Church or the Bible, the Christian faith spells the death of all attempts to codify absolutely Christian life and conduct. *Agape* now governs the Christian and it becomes difficult, if not well-nigh impossible, to settle back on irrevocable systems of rules and regulations. If through Christ the legalism of the Law has been overcome, then no individual Christian or group of Christians has the right to demand of others a certain life-style that conforms to their particular group-image.

But, we may ask, will not this questioning of laws and regulations in the Christian life lead to permissiveness and licence as Christians 'do their own thing'? Of course, such dangers are always present when responsible freedom is being exercised. The nettle must be grasped, however — we are called to follow Christ and no one else. If we have been justified by faith in him, that same doctrine should permeate every feature of the Church and every area of Christian living. This means for us all that we are accepted by God as we are, and we are not expected to ape the standards of others. For the community the implications are no less clear — acceptance must mark all our relationships, codes of behaviour and systems of church government. We are called then to participate in Christ's freedom and in his openness to others, dominated as it was by *agape*.

Is this too easy? If 'love is the fulfilling of the law' this implies that it is never merely easy or simple; on the contrary it is radical and costly, because the character of Christian freedom is the pattern of Jesus Christ in his responsibility to his Father and the world. This kind of responsive love involves holiness, sacrifice and obedience. The Christian who lives like that can never be accused of 'doing his own thing'! Furthermore, far from being lawless it is governed by the Lordship of Christ.

Inevitably, even within the Christian community certain rules or norms need to operate, for the sake of the young Christian in his growth and as constant reminders to all of the standard of Christian living. Even in the vigorous Pauline churches guidelines had to be drawn up for Christian life and conduct. At the end of practically every letter Paul reminded his readers what commitment to Jesus Christ and to one another entailed. Sometimes Paul had to exercise the painful responsibility of discipline. But lest I should be accused of having my cake and eating it in acknowledging the value of rules within the Christian life, I repeat that the 'law of Christ' with its content of love dictated to Paul as it does to us, that rules are always provisional and never absolute. Rules stand, as we do — beneath the cross of Christ and the grace of God.

CHRISTIAN EXISTENCE — A DESIRABLE OPTION?

Our examination of the Christian life has shown that Christ is its pattern, goal and inspiration. When the individual becomes a Christian, Christ comes between him and everything else. In Bonhoeffer's words, 'we cannot establish any contact outside ourselves except through him. He stands in the centre between my neighbour and myself.'[5] A Christian, then, is a Christ-dominated person whose entire life-pattern is dependent upon and controlled by his Lord. But such an existence in which Christ 'stands between' raises the important question concerning the Christian attitude to the world. The Church has never come to a common mind about this problem. One extreme, typified by Tertullian of Carthage, in the early third century, was that the true Christian response is complete withdrawal from the world, except for those things necessary for human existence. According to this view the world is sinful, the sphere of the devil, and the Church is the ark of salvation. The other extreme, represented most clearly by certain sections of the modern Church, is to treat the world as a place in which the Christian should be fully identified because it is God's creation which he loves. To be sure, there are degrees between these two extremes, as Richard Niebuhr's study *Christ and Culture* makes clear, but such variety of opinion supports the point that is being made, that it is not at all self-evident what the Christian response to the world should be and how his 'humanness' should be expressed in it.

The ambivalence of the Christian attitude to the world in which he is set may account for the fact that in the opinion of many non-Christians the Christian idea of humanity is not an attractive form of genuine human existence. Indeed some would say that it is a travesty of genuine humanity, hindering the full development of personality. Friedrich Nietzsche is well known as a bitter adversary of Christianity. Although his highly vitriolic shrill outburst against the Christian faith hints at the insanity which finally engulfed him, we have to remember that he is enunciating what some people believe today. According to him the Christian emphasis upon spirituality and moral behaviour is a war against passion; Christianity overcomes by 'castration', by exterminating human desires. He argues that to attack the passions at their roots means to attack life at its roots; the practice of the Church is hostile to life. He continues later in this same book *The Twilight of the Gods*, 'The saint in whom God takes pleasure is the ideal castrate...life is at an end when the Kingdom of God begins.' Furthermore, 'gloominess' dominates the Christian mind; 'hatred of mind, of pride, courage, freedom, libertinage of mind, is Christian; hatred of the senses, of the joy of the senses, of joy in general, is Christian.' In *The Anti-Christ* Nietzsche concludes his diatribe against Christianity by accusing it of being 'the one great curse, the one great inhuman depravity...the one immoral blemish of mankind'. Why? Because in his opinion it has dehumanised man and made him less than man with its 'slave mentality' and morality. The Christian may retort that both books, written just under a year before Nietzsche went mad, show all the signs of the approaching collapse of his mind, but the question is that, even if Nietzsche's polemic is maniacal, is there sufficient in the charge to substantiate the belief that to be a Christian is to have an unnatural and life-hating existence?

Leaving the question open for the moment, we turn from the charge that the Christian is a eunuch, to the contention that to be a Christian is to be a perpetual child. Sigmund Freud always believed that there was something unnatural in religion in its emphasis upon the human need for God. God, for him, was a father-figure, protective, demanding, an absolute tyrant and an obstacle for the full development of the human ego which, he argued, should struggle stoically through life without the support of such an illusion. Contrary to popular belief, Freud did not deny that religion and Christianity in particular could be valuable, but in his view it was something mankind should outgrow just as a child outgrows the seemingly inevitable neuroses of infancy. Religion, then, for him is the 'universal obsessional neurosis of humanity', and at the heart of the desire to become a Christian is the subconscious search for security and meaning in a hostile and indifferent universe. A Christian girl I know had to visit a psychiatrist for a check-up and was most indignant when she was asked, 'Is your God the kind who leads a blindfolded donkey?' Such was his opinion of Christian experience.

A variation of Freud's critique of the Christian life is the assumption that Christianity is a religion for the weak and not the strong — for children, women and old people; for soft emotions, in fact. Certainly it is not a religion for the man of action; he can find no outlet for his aggressive, assertive energies in its quietness and 'gentle Jesus meek and mild' theology. This criticism is put forward trenchantly in J. C. Flugel's momentous work *Man, Morals and Society*. Flugel, having levelled this criticism, offers Christianity some advice that 'the religious emotions must in their turn be channelled along active and social lines, if they are to serve (and perhaps to save) humanity'.[6] Machiavelli made very much the same kind of charge centuries back when he complained that the

Christian pattern of life appeared to have made the world weak: 'If our religion demands that in you there be strength, what it asks for is strength to suffer rather than strength to do bold things.'

Christianity as 'slave-mentality', as an 'infantile neurosis', as an 'effeminate creed' — and if we add to these Karl Marx's charge that it is an 'opiate' as well, it makes us wonder why Christianity has survived, if such learned men can see it as clearly as that!

All of these approaches *may* be gross over-simplifications of Christian humanity and savage caricatures of its role in society, but there is usually some truth in caricature. Indeed, in these devastating criticisms there is enough accuracy to sting, even if they do not kill. Christianity does often seem dull and lifeless. Its drab respectability can give the superficial impression of a timid, emasculated faith which has lost the dynamism of its youth; now talking in a tired language it appears to have little to offer a modern, bustling world.

These impressions are wrong. The Christian will reply to these charges that to be a Christian is to discover the authentic human existence which can only be known through Christ and his power. There was nothing of the slave mentality in Christ the Lord. On the contrary, we cannot but be amazed and attracted by the nature of his life. No one could accuse him of being less than human; his ministry was completely free and purposeful and people found it easy to respond to his openness and love. In his company individuals began to be changed as he began to influence their thinking and behaviour. But it wasn't only the weak who found his strength. Take the aggressive extroverted Peter (surely one of Flugel's activists!) whose boastful and colourful behaviour masked inner problems no less serious than those whose inadequacies lay nearer the surface. Peter's conversion did not make him less of a man but a better man, more effective and less selfish, less closed-up by an ego-complex; open to others because he was at last open to God. And, of course, one could show quite simply from Christian history the same power for good that Christ has had upon countless individuals and societies. Speaking personally, if in my encounter with Christianity I am supposed to have discovered gloominess,

escapism and a distrust of joy and laughter, I can only say
that my experience has been quite the opposite. I have seen in
Christians certain things that are wrong (but whoever says
Christians are perfect? They would be the first to deny that
idea), but I have also found love, joy, acceptance, peace;
indeed, many of those elements which go to make up the
portrait of integrated people.

In short, the criticisms of such thinkers are grave distortions
based on superficial knowledge of Christianity, whilst coupled
with deep prejudice. Freud's own preoccupation with religion
linked with his life-long rejection of, and attack upon it,
would have made him a suitable study for psycho-analytical
enquiry! We do not deny Freud's great contribution to the
psychology of religion; but his attention to spurious and sick
forms of Christianity leads us to ask, 'If there is neurotic
religion, why not healthy forms as well?' As a psychiatrist
Freud would hardly have come across mature and integrated
Christian experience. And this in turn serves to remind us
that someone who has spent his entire life dealing with the
problems of sick people is hardly the person to give a
balanced and comprehensive view of the healthy life.[7] We
would not expect an expert in geriatrics to be the best
medical advisor to an Olympic athletic team!

The value of such criticism of the Christian life is that it
assists us in working out a doctrine of man that is relevant,
meaningful and appealing to modern people. If our contemporaries are going to be put off Christianity let it be because
of the 'scandal' at the heart of the gospel, not because of false
interpretations by others. Far from Christ calling us to a
weak, over-secure and cushioned existence in the world, to be
a Christian is to live under the shadow of the cross. We agree
with Käsemann's opinion that Christ is more than 'just a coal
carrier who unloads his sack of coal at our back door' meeting
our religious needs.[8] Yes, he does that, and more; he involves
us in his activity of transforming the world and bearing his
cross within it. Faith therefore confers a sense of responsibility
for others and, inevitably, this necessitates that Christians will
attempt 'bold things' for their Lord and his world. We reject
as false, therefore, the assumption that once we are Christians
we are automatically cut off from the world and its needs,

and in our own private ante-room of heaven. To be a Christian, we contend, is to be a genuine human being, because God is now given the chance to make us fully open for him to use in loving and responsible ways in his world. Christians are therefore committed to his world — to care for it, love it, and evangelise it — because they are first committed to him. If this is indicative of a 'slave-mentality' then I for one am happy and proud to be a slave for Christ — because in that condition I am the greatest use for others.

NOTES

1   D. Moberg, *The Great Reversal* (Holman Books, 1972), p. 172.
2   D. Bonhoeffer, *The Cost of Discipleship* (SCM, 1959), p. 79.
3   John Oman, *Grace and Personality* (CUP, 1931), p. 225.
4   D. Bonhoeffer, *Ethics* (Fontana, 1964), p. 252.
5   D. Bonhoeffer, *The Cost of Discipleship*, p. 84.
6   J. C. Flugel, *Man, Morals and Society* (Peregrine Books, 1962), p. 334.
7   For an excellent examination of the psychology of Christian experience, read Giorio Zunini, *Man and his Religion* (Chapman, 1969).
8   E. Käsemann, *Jesus means Freedom* (SCM, 1969), p. 65.

CHAPTER 6

Man in Community

So FAR WE have concentrated upon man as an individual. If as we have suggested, he is cast in God's image, then each person is of inalienable worth to God. This forms the basis of God's desire that individually we should grow into the likeness of Christ, the perfect and complete man.

'No man is an island'

But man cannot survive or grow *in vacuo*. Each of us needs human company if we are to mature as persons. It is doubtful, in fact, if we can speak of a person at all, apart from his relationship and interaction with others. 'People, people who need people, are the luckiest people in the world', sings Barbra Streisand. But more than 'luck' is involved. It is through contact with people — physical, intellectual, emotional and spiritual — that we become aware· of our own personhood. Yet the subtle influences of society are often forgotten. In the thirteenth century Frederick II was eager to discover what language a child might speak if he grew up without being taught the mother tongue. He experimented with some foundling children and instructed the nurses to give the minimum of care and to maintain total silence. The infants died within the first year. Death was caused not through language deprivation but through love deprivation. Frederick failed to realise that words are not the only ways, indeed not even the most important ways, of communicating. Normal everyday living with others consists of a continuous

series of events which *communicate*, often without a word being
exchanged, and through these communications we grow
towards self-understanding as well as appreciation of others.
Any mother knows that you dare not change a baby's nappy
as impersonally as if you were changing a tyre! The hands
that clothe the infant or caress him are not merely performing
useful services but are indirectly allowing him to make his
first feeble explorations of a world which he cannot, as yet,
differentiate clearly from himself.

In the complicated interweaving of relationships human
beings influence and shape one another, and in so doing
change society for good or ill. Of course, society is experienced through different levels of groupings. The family unit
is the first cluster of relationships which mould our life-style.
Thereafter, other influences begin to mix with it — school,
club, church, work — so that the individual stands at the
heart of many varied social relationships, influencing and
being influenced.

Society's influence on man is not always helpful. It can be
extremely harmful. Although the individual and society
interact upon each other, that interaction is not symmetrical.
The range of influence of the individual is usually severely
limited. A man may influence his family very profoundly;
often an individual will have considerable say in the local
community. But few individuals get the opportunity to
influence a nation or to change the world. On the other hand,
society has enormous power to shape and mould individuals.
Of course, what it moulds them into depends to a great extent
upon the nature and characteristics of the society. If it is one
in which freedom is restricted, with education, art and the
media controlled for specific ends, we are not surprised if its
citizens look like programmed people with a common philosophy and similar behaviour patterns. Communist China is
an example. The reverse can also apply: if a society neglects
discipline and moral guidelines, giving the impression that
life is but a 'game' to be enjoyed and not taken too seriously,
we shall not be surprised when debauchery and selfishness,
together with a 'playboy' attitude to life are placed high on
the scale of values.

In general the individual will embody the values, desires

and beliefs of the society which has influenced his growth and development. If we wish men to develop into responsible, mature citizens, society as a whole must demonstrate values it wishes to see reflected in its citizens. It follows, that in a corrupt system of society, with injustice, inequality and a mockery of moral standards, the odds are against a man becoming a truly harmonious self.

It is not only in the area of morals that the influence of society is felt. If, as we believe, human beings need the nourishment of a loving, caring society to enjoy full human lives, the development of industrial society into a dominating impersonal colossus threatens this growth. The individual no longer feels he counts in society; he feels instinctively that it is totally indifferent to who he is and what he does. He is of utility value only. Little wonder modern man is puzzled by his existence, which is reflected in his feelings of personal insignificance, alienation and meaninglessness. Corresponding with this, his three most pressing questions are: Who am I? Where am I? Why am I? These questions come out of the darkness of great bewilderment and heart-searching, and present a challenge to the Christian understanding of man. As we analyse them in more detail, we will try to show that the Christian faith, far from ignoring modern man's dilemmas, is still relevant to his real needs.

1.'WHO AM I?' — THE SEARCH FOR IDENTITY

In the Second World War Nazi administration introduced a decree known as the *Nacht und Nebel* (night and fog) law.[1] By this decree certain persons could be deprived of their identities. Every record concerning them — birth and wedding certificates, insurance policies, and other personal documents — would be destroyed. Henceforth, they would exist only as numbers. In addition, to prevent them forming close relationships, they would be constantly on the move from camp to camp. For the unfortunate victim the message was terribly clear: 'as far as life is concerned you are non-existent; a non-person. You are the living dead and no trace of you will ever remain.'

I am not suggesting for a moment that this hell is

paralleled in Western culture. This would clearly be false; very often the message is reiterated that the individual is important and his personal status is of great consequence. However, even if the *Nacht und Nebel* decree belonged to a particularly evil spot in the history of humanity, the pressures of modern society are almost as effective in undermining the sense of personal identity, resulting in disorientation and confusion.

To begin with, we are often told we live in an age of change, but the startling effect of rapid change upon the individual has only been appreciated in the last few years. The creation of new highways, tower blocks, apartments, sports centres — advantageous as they are — may so easily have the negative effect of weakening the individual's sense of belonging, because the alteration of his environment cuts him off from his past. Separated from his origins he is part of a frantic everchanging 'now'. Rootless, he is aware of the impermanence of everything and of his own insignificance. The term 'throw-away' society, invented by man, becomes a symbol of man.

The question 'who am I?' also arises from the breakdown of community. Many of the people we meet in the course of a day are strangers about whom we know nothing, and after a brief encounter they pass from us for ever, still unknown. Business is rarely conducted in the context and interests of community, but is usually expressed in bald economic transactions. Try as we may to overcome the forces of depersonalisation, all our attempts seem futile. As a token gesture, the girl behind the counter at the bank is given a name tag to wear; our business is personalised — we are dealing with Miss Smith! But it is a hollow pretence — to what extent is it possible to know anything about Miss Smith apart from her name? Attempts to 'chat her up' or to lean across the counter to discuss the weather, politics, or her father's health would be courteously discouraged.

The search for identity is therefore an important quest in the modern world. Mass society triumphs over community but the price is individual significance. Of course, many are glad to pay the price. Significant or insignificant, they are not too bothered as long as they can get on with the job of living.

But the issue cannot be ducked like that. If a man is to live a full human existence in society, he must live as a significant person within it, not as a slave existing on 'hand-outs'.

Ironically, the question 'who am I?' occurs in the context of great freedom. Never before has man been as free to express himself. In matters of morals, and travel, he has unlimited freedom and scope to discover his identity; in spite of this he is perhaps more imprisoned than ever within society, because of its complexity. Our highly-skilled technology demands ever-increasing specialisation in which freedom to change the direction of one's career is very difficult — in spite of retraining programmes. So when unemployment comes it brings pain and bitterness. More than a job is involved, a person's self-respect and sense of significance comes under attack. The now-familiar story of the student parading the placard, 'I am a person, do not spindle, tear or mutilate', is a modern protest against de-personalisation. People do not want to be highly-qualified ciphers in amorphous and impersonal companies, they know inwardly they have a significance which transcends their impersonal roles.

God as a Father

Against this background, the Christian message of man's significance before God is of immense importance. 'Fear not, for I have redeemed you. I have called you by name, you are mine' (Isa. 43:1). That the Creator should speak of man like that is staggering and only really credible in the light of Christ's person and work. Indeed, it is to him we must look to discover what man means to God, because in describing God as Father (*Abba*) he introduced a completely new dimension to the relationship between God and man. The Old Testament and contemporary Judaism were very reluctant to speak of God as 'father'. Only fourteen times in the Old Testament is God addressed in this way (e.g. Jer. 3:44; 3:18; Mal. 1:6; Isa. 64:8). Likewise, the Jews at the time of Christ occasionally addressed God as 'father' but never in a personal way. Jeremias observes, 'To date nobody has produced one single instance in Palestinian Judaism where God is addressed as "My Father" by an individual person.'[2] And yet this was

Jesus's normal practice. What is most significant is that he employs the Aramaic word *Abba*. *Abba* was the word that a Jewish child would use of his earthly father, a simple childish term that summed up a precious intimacy. *Abba* and *Imma* — daddy and mummy — were then, as they are today, the first words a little child would utter. To many Jews with their pronounced emphasis upon the transcendence and 'otherness' of God, the idea of using such a term would be unthinkable and irreverent, bordering on blasphemy. Jeremias continues, 'It was something new, something unique and unheard of, that Jesus dared to take this step to speak with God as a child with his father, simply, intimately, securely.'[3]

This practice was not a thing that Jesus kept to himself. He encouraged his disciples to follow his example and to see the Fatherhood of God at the centre of human existence (Luke 11:1-13; Matt. 5:43-48). Paul also in a flash of profound insight makes *Abba* the centre of the living experience of God as Father, Son and Spirit: 'Because you are sons, God has sent the Spirit of his Son into our hearts crying "Abba! Father!" ' (Gal. 4:6).

Not for Jesus, then, nor for his followers was God an impersonal deity, removed from human concerns and distress. On the contrary, at the heart of Jesus's teaching is the conviction that his 'Abba-God' cares for all men to the point of being intensely concerned with the well-being of each individual. Inevitably the value he gave to humanity brought him into collision with the thinking of his day. He rejected society's domination of man expressed as it was then in the importance of cherished institutions; 'The Sabbath', he declared, 'was made for man, not man for the Sabbath' (Mark 2:28). In his challenge to the interpretation of the Law he was giving voice to the protest that man must not be imprisoned by the over-pricing of tradition, or for that matter, religious or secular legalism. He reassured men of God's providence and care day by day. 'Even the hairs of your head are numbered' (Matt. 10:30) is his graphic illustration of God's concern. God is interested in the daily timetable of each person's life, not just his religious activities. His interest goes much further than a mere knowledge of us as persons; he cares for man's physical and spiritual needs.

Hence the teaching that runs through the Gospels that God, who clothes the lilies of the field, will clothe his people; the one who feeds the ravens will feed us. Furthermore, in the Prayer to our Father (the common title, the *Lord's prayer*, while correct, detracts from the theme of the prayer) the basis of Christ's assurance that our daily needs will be met is the fatherly activity of God in his world.

At the heart of Christianity, then, there is the assertion that in God's sight the individual has an identity that makes him distinctive and special as a person. God says of each person, 'There is no one quite like you in my creation. I made you, called you into being and named you. You belong to me.' It is not surprising that many people who have lost sight of their identity as individuals have found in this simple teaching a discovery of God's love beyond their wildest dreams. What is more, this teaching is radical; it cuts right against the drift of secular thinking. So Charles Mayer, a declared unbeliever, admits the stark difference between the Christian view of man and his own: 'If man is not God's creation but only the outcome of a long evolution with a fortuitous origin, then his value is of a purely utilitarian order. His worth lies only in what he is.'[4] What a contrast!

Father of All?

Is God the Father of all mankind, or is he the Father of a few exclusive people who have the luck to hear and respond to the gospel? This is not a theological question irrelevant to our subject; it is absolutely basic to it, because our entire approach as Christians to non-Christians and to the world revolves around the answer we give. Many will respond by replying that God is only Father to those who are redeemed. Indeed, a formidable array of texts is marshalled to support their case. Did not Jesus say that 'no one knows the Father except the Son and anyone to whom the Son chooses to reveal him' (Matt. 11:27)? Didn't he distinguish between different origins when he rebuked the Jews 'you are of your father the Devil' (John 8:44)? Appeal is also made to Paul who, in Ephesians, distinguishes between being by nature 'children of wrath' (Eph. 2:3) and 'destined in love to be his sons through

Jesus Christ' (1:5). On the other hand, there are those who assert that God's Fatherhood is universal and not restricted to the redeemed. Proponents of this view often start from the basis of God's love in Christ: 'Isn't the offer of Christ's salvation to all men an indirect argument that God is Father of all, who is unwilling that his children should perish?' Appeal is also made to scripture which seems to support this view: 'He made from one every nation of men to live on all the face of the earth...for we are indeed his offspring' (Acts 17:26; cf. Eph. 3:15).

In point of fact the two apparently irreconcilable positions may be harmonised quite easily if we distinguish between different understandings of Fatherhood. Bearing in mind the image of three concentric circles we may be able to separate three quite different but united concepts of sonship and Fatherhood. The first and smallest of the circles is the unique Father-son relationship between God and Jesus. Jesus is son by nature; or to use theological jargon he is son 'ontologically'. His sonship denotes a relationship with God too profound and intimate for mortals to share or appreciate. Outside the first circle, representing this unique relationship, we can draw a second circle representing the adopted sonship which is ours through faith in Christ. Adopted, yes, but nevertheless a real sonship and we can join our Lord in crying 'Abba! Father!' The Christian belongs to the family of God and has access into God's presence with the freedom that any human child has with his normal father. Now he lives in an environment of love, built around God's grace in Christ.

The third and largest of our circles is mankind separated from God through sin and disobedience but never, never, separated from the claims and desires of his love. Alienated and 'children of wrath' they may be, but this does not make them any less children of God. Cannot wrath and judgment be understood as fatherly concepts? The only thing that stops God's wrath from being cruel, capricious and sub-human is that it proceeds from a heart that loves his children, and that longs for them to turn to him. Unredeemed men, we argue, are children of God by creation although cut off from the life of the family through sin. Yet the love of the Father pursues them. This, after all, is the theme of the Parable of the

Prodigal Son. (Luke 15). It is clear that in the story the prodigal represents lost people in general (v. 1) and through the narrative he is viewed as a son who will surely perish unless he returns to God. This he does and he is joyfully reclaimed by the father. At this point, of course, the prodigal child really becomes a son in the sense that he behaves as one, by entering once more into relationship with his father and into the life of the family. He passes, so to speak, from the third circle, to the second.

This picture may help us see all mankind from God's perspective. If his love and fatherly care reaches to all men, who are we to impose barriers on others or give them a lower value than the one we believe God gives us?

Persons or Conditioned Reflexes?

If then we are children of one heavenly Father we have in our relationship with him a model for all relationships, not only within the Church but outside it as well. At the centre of this model is the love and unstinting sacrifice of God's quest for his creatures to enter freely and gladly into a richer and deeper relationship with him. It is this love which must characterise our relationships with each other. The vertical relationship to God and the horizontal relationship to our brothers are to be seen as opposite sides of the same coin. So the Epistle of John shows the connection in the trenchant remark, 'If anyone says "I love God" and hates his brother, he is a liar' (1 John 4:20). To belong to God is to belong to others, because we are made members of his family. The more a person realises the significance of his relationship to God the more he will grow aware of his need for others and the personal relationship that now exists between himself and others. It is no accident that in Jesus's teaching the question of human relationships is treated as a spiritual issue. In the Gospel of Luke, especially, social relationships are seen as crucial elements of Christian discipleship. Christ is shown as one who goes out of his way to establish links with the deprived and the non-persons of Jewish society. Whether they are the poor, children, women, slaves, lepers, or Samaritans, Jesus is seen as one who treats them as persons of dignity, worthy of respect because they are children of God and fully able to respond to the love of God.

Inevitably, the Christian model of relationships in society is at variance with many secular theories. We may consider as an example the influential neo-behaviourist school led by B. F. Skinner. According to Skinner, man is neither good nor bad but merely a bundle of conditioned reflexes. The individual behaves in this way or that way because he has been taught by reward or punishment to do so. 'Autonomous' man does not exist; a person's life is controlled by environmental conditioning. Our patterns of behaviour, says Skinner, are determined by reinforcement of particular actions by repetition — 'operant conditioning' he calls it. He distinguishes between two forms of reinforcement; positive reinforcement whose effects are beneficial, and negative reinforcement which, obviously, has aversive effects.[5]

In his popular novel *Walden II* Skinner gives us a glimpse of social engineering and how conditioning techniques might lead to an enlightened society. One passage in the book describes children arriving back at the community hungry and tired after a long walk. As a lesson in self-control they are ordered to stand for five minutes in front of hot, appetising bowls of soup. Complaints or groans of dismay are treated as 'wrong answers'. Unwanted behaviour is eliminated by positive reinforcers — firmness, control, encouragement — which lead to the desired response. Traditional forms of punishment are treated as negative reinforcers and inefficient methods of controlling behaviour. Thus, Skinner's deliberate aim is that educational and learning techniques should be programmed to produce better citizens and a better society.

While much is helpful in Skinner's understanding of human nature and society, much is alien to Christian teaching. It is clear that Skinner has little sense of the importance of the individual. He is almost completely subordinated to society; merely a blank slate on which society may write as it wishes. Very few people would wish to deny the immense influence exerted by society over the individual, nor would we wish to resist forms of education which would eliminate evil from human society. But it is an enormous jump from that view to Skinner's rejection of individual personhood. Three obvious objections stand out.

First, we can agree with Skinner that the concept of an 'autonomous' self is a myth. There is no such thing as an autonomous self, a secure, protected 'I', immune and un-affected by society. In fact, 'autonomous' man is a myth created by Skinner who thinks that this is what most people believe. We all acknowledge the shaping influence of our environment, the enormous powers it exerts in its social and cultural forms. But this is a far cry from saying that we are the passive pliable 'plasticine' upon which the finger of society works. Skinner's thesis is surprisingly close to the empiricism of David Hume (d. 1776) who also attacked the idea of a self. But as Immanuel Kant pointed out long ago in reaction against Hume, the mind actively transforms sense data into intelligible reality. In other words, though each one of us is affected and influenced by environment, none of us is enslaved by it — we are free to choose, create and organise. So the anthropologist René Dubos comes into inadvertent conflict with Skinner when he writes: 'Within the controls imposed by the biological determinant of his nature, man can make responsible choices. He has the privilege and responsi-bility of shaping his self and his future.'[6]

Secondly, Skinner ignores genetic factors in his concentra-tion upon environment. To be sure, the development which takes place in every individual transcends his hereditary legacy, but we know also that his genetic endowment inevitably affects his encounter with other people. The rich and complex variety of genetic influences has profound repercussions upon the conditioning technique of the 'Skinner box' which assumes equal responses from people. Further-more Skinner by-passes psychological factors. Human beings are not 'equal' psychologically speaking and it is no good pretending they are. Skinner's positive programming could well have alarming effects on the weak and perhaps neglible effects on the strong.

Finally, it is not at all clear, if Skinner's views were to undergird our educational and social thinking, who would 'programme our programmers'! And we would dearly love to know what would be the content and aim of the programme!

All we know is that untold possibility for evil as well as good lie in this theory. We need only look back to Nazism to see that manipulative techniques are soon separated from a neutral philosophy to form unholy alliances with evil ideologies.

2. 'WHERE AM I?' — THE STRUGGLE AGAINST ALIENATION

The question '*where* am I?' is the puzzled cry of the alienated person and it is the inevitable result of the loss of identity brought about by the modern world. There are different forms of alienation which make intelligent people question their place within society. 'Where am I?' asks the shopper as she wheels her trolley down the narrow passages between shelves stacked with enticements to buy, while piped music lulls her into hypnotic acceptance of their message of plenty. As a person she is a 'nobody' and of little value, as an abstract customer she is important. She is alienated from those who sell.

'Where am I?' asks the workman, drilling holes in pieces of metal which come past at the rate of ten a minute. He cannot point proudly to his work — a washing machine, car, or a cabinet — and say 'I made that'. His contribution was probably infinitesimal and he is aware of it. He is alienated from his work and finds little satisfaction in it. This is reflected in the relationship between employer and employee which these days is normally an economic relationship only. On the one hand the employer employs people as he would employ a machine — they are commodities used to get greater productivity. On the other hand, the employee uses his boss in the same way for self-interest. They are bound together, not by sentiments of pride in fine craftsmanship, but by the harsh realities of a profit motive. Each is using the other for gain. The advice given to young men going into business that 'the only way to get on is to sell yourself' points to the way persons are assumed to be commodities, similar to any other expendable item. Little wonder that many people feel frustrated and ask, 'what am I apart from my utility value? Where do I fit into this society which needs my gifts or money but not me?'

Alienation also occurs in political areas. The growth of society with a corresponding growth of communication between the individual and his public representatives often results in deep frustration. The feeling that our point of view cannot be heard and that we cannot influence policy can lead to personal disorientation. Two dangers may result from this sense of uncertainty. The first is a 'head in the sand' attitude which refuses to recognise the growing chasm taking place. This policy of withdrawal is often accompanied by a corresponding retreat into pseudo-religions which offer a man security, or into pleasures which take his mind off real life. The other danger is that frustrated individuals, alienated from society, may feel that the only real solution left is to turn against it and work for a total change in philosophy and constitution. Hence alienation becomes the stuff of revolution.

Marxism and the longing for Utopia

'The optimist proclaims that we live in the best of all possible worlds and the pessimist fears it is true,' goes the saying. But there is a widespread longing for a golden age on earth when wrongs will be put right and when human dignity and justice will prevail. This desire was behind many of the journeys to the New World.

Utopias have, of course, been written to illustrate many different theories of the perfect society. In J. V. Andreae's *Christianopolis* (1619) the secret of the Utopian society is true religion; in William Morris's *News from Nowhere* (1890) a socialist society is set up as the model; one in which all are helpful, tolerant, kind and unselfish and sharing. The basis for a new society is education, according to Samuel Gott's *New Jerusalem* (1648); whereas in *New Atlantis* (1626) by Francis Bacon there is a touching faith in the blessings of science.

In the modern period the Utopian vision of Karl Marx has gripped the imagination of secular man. It appears to provide a rational and realistic programme for a better world. Central to this programme was Marx's idea that alienation was the root problem in industrial society. Alienation had to be eradicated to free man from his modern prison. But how did Marx arrive at his concept of alienation? He was indebted to two thinkers, Ludwig Feuerbach and Moses Hess who influenced him in two separate ways. First Feuerbach's man-centred philosophy struck him as being the back-bone of a new society. 'Nothing exists outside man,' announced Feuerbach, 'and the higher beings our religious fantasia have created are only the fantastic reflections of our own essence.'[7] Here is the death of God with a vengeance. God is made in man's image and not the other way about! He exists only in human thought, feelings and hopes. Religion was to Feuerbach a form of alienation from which man must emancipate himself if he wants to be truly human. To this thesis Marx added the insights he derived from Moses Hess, that money represents alienated man, because it is the symbol of the labour and productivity captured by egotistical and unscrupulous men who hold others in their power.

As Marx's thinking developed he saw that man's alienation lies in three main forms. First, he is alienated from the product of his own labour because in industrial society it does not belong to him. The more value he creates, the more valueless he becomes. He works for the gain of others and his products become symbols of his slavery. Secondly, man is alienated from his work because of industrialisation. According to Marx, the division of labour leading to varying forms of specialisation degrades man, making him a servant. Thirdly, because of the capitalist system the worker is alienated within a 'class' society; a society dominated by the idols of money and possessions in which the worker, without whom wealth would be impossible, has but a tiny share.

Karl Marx was a visionary. Although his theory of productivity would of itself have accorded him an honourable place in the history of ideas, it is as an artist and dreamer that we should view him. Skilfully compiling and weaving social history into the framework of his vision, he gave to the world a new myth to account for man's bondage. In this myth, a new religion for modern man, there are two main characters, a hero called the Proletariat and a villain named the Capitalist. The hero finds himself imprisoned by the villain and despicably used by him. Although in chains, the hero is growing in strength all the time. History will approach its final act when the Proletariat rises up to break his chains and overcome Capitalism, to be free at last.

In spite of the noble dream of a society in which man will be liberated from bondage, oppression, fear and want, Marx's secular Utopia faces many grave objections. Intellectually, it is generally regarded as being completely unconvincing, even if politically it is still plausible to many. Let us consider a few objections to his viewpoint.

To begin with, industrial alienation is not obliterated by the elimination of capitalists! Marx failed to distinguish between alienation which belongs to a political and economic system and that which is part of the structure of working conditions. Is the workman who presses a button ten thousand times a day in Stalingrad any more integrated and whole than his counterpart in Pittsburg, Sheffield or the Ruhr? No: in each there may be found deep-rooted alienation if he has not come to terms with his working conditions. No amount of recitation of shibboleths will remove irritations which are present whatever political systems may be adopted. A change of ownership can effect very little while industrialism remains untouched and while the individual is ignored.

For all his horror at the oppression of humanity, Marx seems to ignore the individual. Although he looks forward to the creation of the coming Communist society in which the individual will be fulfilled, and which will provide a complete solution to all his needs and problems, it must be emphasised that significance is given to the individual only in terms of his representative function as a bearer of society. It is as a 'species being' that the individual will obtain liberation. Ultimately then, there is little scope for attributing significance to the individual, because it is the secular state that is regarded as all-important. The individual is significant only in so far as he embodies the ideas of society. Indeed one charge that we must level at Marxism is that because of its idealisation of 'humanity' yet neglect of the individual, it has behaved with a frightening moral indifference to human rights and suffering. We rightly condemn Nazism for its inhumanity to the Jews, yet at least as many people died in Russian prison camps before the last war.

Is it true that by rectifying the social and economic inequalities between men, the needs of men will be satisfied? Surely not; much of man's alienation goes a lot deeper. Even if Marx's dream of the Communist society were to be realised, man would still be a problem to himself because he would be aware of forms of alienation untouched by the revolution. Marx naïvely supposed that men are basically good. All that is needed to change man's position is to change his institution and his political system. Once this is done and economic exploitation removed, the free, classless society will come into being. But the problem of man's alienation cannot be solved that simply. It is highly probable that even within the Communist society man would still be a problem to himself, knowing contradictions within, and unfulfilled in his personal life. Indeed, the irony of Marxism is that the post-revolutionary institutions clearly demand 'perfect' people to lead them and work in them. 'Nothing in contemporary thought is finally quite so Utopian as Marxism', charges Leslie Paul.[8] Christians are sometimes accused of proclaiming 'pie in the sky when we die'; events have shown that the man-centred philosophy of Marx has certainly not succeeded in supplying much 'pie on earth'. The tragedy of Marx was that in expelling God from his thought he only solved a small part of man's alienation.

God's Kingdom

In the face of the tremendous problems which face humanity today it may seem naïve and somewhat quaint that we should mention the idea of the Kingdom. Nevertheless, Jesus's programme of introducing the Kingdom is still the goal to which the Christian is committed.

What is this Kingdom? And why are we committed to it? The short answer is that it was the central theme of Christ's teaching. Initially, this was not considered particularly remarkable because in the first century all Jews longed for the coming of the Kingdom of God and it was on the lips of many teachers. What was astonishing about Jesus's news, however, was his assertion that the Kingdom was present in his person. Fancy an unknown, ignorant carpenter from Galilee proclaiming that! Little wonder that to the rabbis his teaching was offensive. But it was clear from his actions as well as his words that Jesus regarded his ministry as being in part God's invasion of human society to establish his Kingdom. The early chapters of Mark's Gospel spell out the force of this counter-revolution: Jesus's authoritative teaching (1: 21-30); his power over evil spirits (1:27); his conquest of disease (1:29-2: 5), and his power to forgive sin (2:2-12).

Yet, in spite of the importance of this message on the lips of Jesus, nowhere does he give a definitive explanation of its meaning and significance. We are left with numerous clues from which we must draw our own conclusions. Three elements stand out for special mention and together they give us some idea how Jesus interpreted the Kingdom.

Firstly, to most of us the word 'Kingdom' usually expresses a territory or place over which a King reigns. But the Hebrew word *malkuth*, when used of God, does not denote a territory but his active rule over his people. It describes the living God acting in his royal power, visiting and redeeming his people, and uniting them to himself. Because God claims them as his own, they belong to his Kingdom.

Secondly, Jesus claimed that God's rule was a present reality in his ministry: 'If it is by the finger of God that I cast out demons, then the Kingdom of God has come upon you' (Luke 11:14). Where Jesus is, there is the Kingdom of God. He is its key and he has unlocked the door so that mankind may step into it. This, of course, means that the Kingdom has a social aspect to it as well as a personal element. If God rules, he must rule over a people, and that body consists of those who love and follow Christ. The community aspect of the Kingdom is well brought out in many of Jesus's parables. The 'Kingdom-parables' of the mustard seed, drag-net, and the wheat and tares, reveal that it is a reality that followers of Christ belong to in company with other believers.

But the Kingdom is more than just a present reality. It is abundantly clear that God's Kingdom is not yet fully established but awaits its completion. 'Fear not, little flock,' says Christ to his followers, 'It is your Father's good pleasure to give you the Kingdom' (Luke 12:32). This sets out admirably the tension between present and future aspects of the Kingdom. The Kingdom is here now. It impinges on the world as people follow Christ and serve him. It comes into human existence stealthily, gently and surely, making inroads into human society and transforming its values in the process. This same Kingdom, however, will come in all its fullness as the completion of all things, when Christ delivers the Kingdom to his Father, having conquered all opposing forces (1 Cor. 15:24).

The importance of the Kingdom for our world is tremendous. The Christian Church does not possess a tidy five-year plan by which it seeks to work out God's agenda, but God's Kingdom remains the hope and inspiration of all Christian activity in the world. As a present reality it deals with man's alienation, because it offers a solution here and now to his frustrations. In other words, if man is now a member of God's Kingdom and in fellowship with his Lord and other members of the Body, he has in this framework something which transcends his human existence and which puts everything into perspective.

This means that we must reject Utopianism, because the future coming of the Kingdom reminds us that the idea of setting up a perfect society on earth is 'pipe-dreaming'. But the Christian's aim is to bring human society under the rule of God and so prepare the way for the final triumph of God. We therefore acknowledge the provisional quality of all that we see, but we should not make the mistake of thinking that because it is provisional and transitory it is therefore not worth the effort of doing anything about human society. Many Christians have fallen into this trap. On the contrary, the present must be seen as possessing great potential for Christian people, not only to reflect the presence of the Kingdom, but also to reveal its values and its power to unite alienated men. The Kingdom comes when lives begin to open to the claims of Christ and surrender to him; it comes also when God's peace, love, joy and righteousness are reflected in human society; it comes as the bonds of alienation are cut from the lives of men. We do not claim that Christianity has a monopoly of peace, joy and holiness, but we do assert that in Christ, God's Kingdom comes in a very special and final form. It belongs to the nature of the Christian community to continue his work and await his final victory.

3. 'WHY AM I?' — THE CRY FOR MEANING

Closely linked with man's search for identity and significance in society is his feeling that life ought to have some
form of intelligible pattern and meaning. Yet, so often events
in modern society threaten to make worthless the values of
individual existence. Many tyrants have arisen in human
history, but few have had as much success as the modern state
and big business-combines in robbing individual existence of
meaning. How can an individual find meaning when some
unknown and inaccessible government official somewhere
authorisies a road through his back garden, or changes his
environment beyond recognition, or forces him out of his
home which is now in a 'redevelopment area'? What meaning
may be found in individual existence when, through a mad
frenzy on the Stock Exchange, thousands are made redun-
dant and many ruined? Furthermore, the rapid changes
taking place in the modern world seem to reduce the efforts of
the individual to futility. Everything appears to have temporary significance only. 'Life doesn't add up', remarked a
bewildered and distressed man after enduring the combination of redundancy and eviction in the same week. It is easy
to sympathise with that man's point of view when our aims in
life are frustrated by social forces beyond our control. At
times like these the question 'why?' is uppermost on our
minds.

We know, of course, that the search for purpose is part of
what it means to be human. All the achievements of
humanity have been built on the question 'why?'. It is the
basis of our scientific knowledge, and our religious faith. It is
no accident, however, that it is in our industrial, civilised,
world that existential philosophy has arisen. Modern existentialism is distinguished from other forms of philosophy by its
concentration upon man himself and in particular with the
question of the meaning of human existence. Man the
enquirer becomes man enquired into. At one and the same
time he is both above and below the microscope.

Although there are secular as well as religious types of
existentialism, there is a common emphasis upon the primacy
of the individual and his existence as a person. It is

impossible, within the compass of a wide-ranging book, to give a comprehensive account of this form of philosophy which would do justice to the complex and personal questions raised. But essentially existentialism searches for authentic human existence, asking such questions as : 'How may we live meaningfully?' and 'What is the nature and goal of human existence?'

Some existentialists — like Kierkegaard, Marcel, and K. Jaspers — place God at the heart of human experience and centre the question of meaning in the relationship between God and the person. But for secular existentialists, such as Jean-Paul Sartre and Albert Camus, the affirmation of God undermines man's freedom of choice and therefore his full humanity. Man must break free of the shackles of religion in order to enjoy authentic human existence. But the price of this, Sartre warns, is 'meaninglessness', because only God, in the final analysis, can give meaning to existence. 'The existentialist finds it extremely embarrassing that God does not exist, for there disappears with him all possibility of finding values in an intelligible heaven...everything is indeed permitted if God does not exist.'[9] Here is man's dilemma. Without God he is free, but he is also forlorn and absurd; a 'useless passion' to quote Sartre again.[10] Free and responsible, yes, but alone in a meaningless universe. This is man's grim fate if there is no God to supply the framework of meaning. Camus's philosophy has a different starting point but a similar conclusion. He wrote: 'Man should rectify in creation everything that can be rectified. And after he has done so, children will still die unjustly in a perfect society. Even by his greatest effort, man can only propose to diminish, arithmetically, the sufferings of the world. But the injustice and the suffering of the world will remain and, no matter how limited they are, they will not cease to be an outrage. Dimitri Karamazov's cry of "Why?"' will continue to resound through history.'[11]

The raw nerve exposed by such existentialists is echoed in modern literature. Franz Kafka's novels explore sensitively the mystery of human life. In *The Castle* he describes the efforts of a man who wants to get in touch with the mysterious inhabitants of a castle who are supposed to show him his place in the world and tell him what to do. Yet, in spite of his attempts to meet them, he never succeeds and he is left alone with a sense of utter futility. Joseph Heller has portrayed the same dilemma. In both *Catch 22* and *Something Happened* the purposelessness of life is expressed savagely and cruelly. The difference in technique˙ between Kafka and Heller may be likened to that between a surgeon and a butcher; but with both writers the object is the same — man and his dilemma. In *Catch 22*, a 'comic strip' of lust and carnage, we are shown man at war. Yossarian, the 'hero' of the book, and his comrades are members of an American airforce base on a small island off Italy. Try as they may to get off the island and out of the war, they cannot. Every time they fulfil their quota of missions they are given more. That is 'Catch 22'. Disgust, despair, futility and nihilism pervade the book. The high level of humour should not blind us to its unmistakable message — that nothing is sacred and no relationship is worthwhile. Indeed, the sensual replaces sexual, lust supplants love, and self-preservation is substituted for justice and honour.

In Heller's second book, *Something Happened*, peacetime man is considered; yet a very similar picture of human nature is given. In this massive book the only recognisable plot, such as it is, is that Bob Slocum, a young executive, is promoted. Yet such is the character of this exceptional book, that even this minimal thread becomes a gripping focus of interest. Heller's thesis appears to be that human nature cannot live with its own species without seeking to destroy it; fear dominates. So Bob Slocum comments on his family; 'In the family where I live, there are four people of whom I am afraid. Three of the four people are afraid of me, and each of them is also afraid of the other two. Only one member of our family is not afraid of any of the others and that one is an idiot.' Slocum's self-disgust is plain to see; his relationship to his wife, children and many mistresses is meaningless and tenuous. Yet his self-analysis is honest and correct; 'There are things going on inside me I cannot control and do not admire.' In his opinion no answer to humanity's sickness can be found. 'Smut and weaponry are two areas in which we've improved. Everything else has gotten worse...the face of the rich and the poor age from nativity into the same cramped, desiccated lines of meanness and discontent. People between rich and poor radiate uneasiness. They don't know where they belong!' So Slocum yearns for innocence; 'When I grow up I want to be a little boy.'

Of course, not everyone wrestles with the problem of meaning. Many of our contemporaries hardly question, as far as we can tell, whether life is intelligible or not. On the whole they appear content to settle for meaning in their jobs, homes and families and in the regular patterns of social life. However satisfying these may be, rapid social changes are shaking such areas of meaning. The 'head-in-the-sand' escape route is an exercise few can indulge in comfortably these days. Schiller's famous question, 'Is the universe friendly?' is one we are forced to ask, even if we lack the ability or interest to explore the question philosophically. Population explosion, increasing famine, moral disintegration, declining values, ever-increasing violence, manipulation of the individual — all these things, and more, force themselves within the purview of all men, and require a Christian response.

THE BODY OF CHRIST

If the Christian Church is, as Christians claim, the community in which true freedom, growth and fulfilment become possible, it is obvious that its life and mission are of the greatest relevance to the disintegrated world in which we live. Indeed, God's response to the challenge of a divided and bewildered world is the presence of his people. They embody his presence in the world. Unfortunately, as we know only too well, the Church fails so often to show the reality of God's Kingdom. Apart from spluttering half-heartedly into life twice a week, it gives the impression of being quite irrelevant to this bustling world in which individuals search for indentity and meaning.

What, then, is the role of the Christian Church in society today? Three areas of relevance stand out, in relation to the question of meaning, that give the Christian body a significance and importance unparalleled in the world.

The Church as the creator of community

It was Ferdinand Tönnies who pointed out as long ago as 1887 that the effect of industrialisation was the breakdown of the basic human unit of community (*Gemeinde*) into 'associations' (*Gesellschaften*).[12] By this he meant that within a community man found for himself fulfilment as a person. The self-contained life of the pre-industrial community gave the individual significance, status and a role. But industrialisation, according to Tönnies, led to the disintegration of community and the fragmentation of life, so that a man might live in one place, work in yet another town, and seek his cultural and leisure pursuits in a different place altogether.

Whether or not it is at all possible for modern society to return to the basic unit, it is true that the Christian body is called to be God's community in the world. Yet, too often it exists like an 'association' of like-minded people — a kind of spiritual super-market to which religious people go for a special type of 'pick-me-up'. This is a far cry from the vigorous and creative church life of the New Testament. There may have been a great deal wrong with the church at Corinth to provoke Paul's letters; after all, not every church has such glaring problems of immorality, licence, disunity, drunkenness, greed, and so on. But it is also just as apparent that the same church had a greater intimacy and a deeper level of sharing than most modern Christians have ever encountered. An imperfect community, to be sure, but at least a community — warts and all! Bonhoeffer accurately defined the nature of the Christian community when he described it as 'community through Jesus Christ and in Jesus Christ. No Christian community is more or less than that.' The centrality of Christ is stressed in Paul's definition of the Church as the 'Body of Christ'. He did not mean, of course, that the Church is literally his body but that in it his life is manifested. As his body it is commissioned to exist for others in self-giving service, and to be the place where divided individuals may become fulfilled persons. To use a term that is now familiar jargon since the Vietnam war, the community of Jesus Christ should be the 'liberated zone' where the freedom and power of Christ creates genuine acceptance and love.

This should be the vision and goal of every church. In every place and in every generation its duty is to extend its life so that it may be a real fellowship where individuals find meaning for life, experiencing the love and joy of Christ. It should be possible for the non-Christian world to remark, as Tertullian reported they did of the early Church, 'See how these Christians love one another'.[13] Or, as the pagan Emperor Julian once remarked, 'Why do we not observe that it is their (Christians') benevolence to strangers, their care for the graves of the dead, and the "pretended" holiness of their lives that has done most to increase atheism (Christianity)...it is disgraceful that when no Jew has to beg, and the impious Galilaeans (Christians) support not only their poor, but ours as well, all men see that our people lack aid from us.'[14]

The Church then is called to be a community of meaning in the world, extending its influence and bearing courageous witness to its Lord who calls all men to follow him. This means it is not committed to be an eccentric community, unrelated to life and cut off from its challenges, but *ex-centric*, in that its task is to go out from Christ the centre. Above all, it is a community of meaning to the individual who should find in its fellowship and loving acceptance the means of growth towards maturity. Embodying Christ's love, the Church faces the daunting challenge of invading a society devoid of 'meaning' with the hope and encouragement of a Gospel which leaves no one out.

The Church must affirm the claims and values of God

It is so very easy for a Church to become a ghetto-community with its own culture, U-language and interests, becoming in time indifferent to life outside the 'ghetto'. But the true community of God, if it is going to be a local sign of the presence and activity of God, will be brought into situations where it must represent the value of God's Kingdom firmly but courteously. The risks are enormous, as the ministry of Jesus shows. He overthrew the values of his day and asserted the importance of the individual for God. The unpopularity of his message, in fact, contributed in no small part to his crucifixion. The risks are enormous for us because of the delicate balance between a negative attitude which may suggest a 'you are wrong and we condemn you' approach, and a more positive affirming stance which includes a constructive policy for the attention of others. Yet, although the Christian community must steer a careful course, it must not shirk the responsibility it has been given to be a light in the world (Matt. 5:14). This will involve protests against secular values which dehumanise man and bring him into new forms of bondage.

A very large part of this element of affirming God's standards springs from the Christian evaluation of man. If, as we have stressed, the individual is important to God then the Christian community cannot be indifferent when the life of man is endangered by groups within society which, by changing laws or influencing popular opinion, threaten the very sacredness of human existence. Such issues of crucial importance today are abortion and euthanasia. But the wise Christian will not fall into the trap of thinking that such issues are 'open-and-shut' issues, neither will he adopt a kind of 'finger-in-the-dyke' attitude which suggests that only the Christian Church has the answer. He will recognise that physical, mental, spiritual and sociolcgical considerations are invariably intertwined in such issues and he will want to plead for flexibility. Yet, having said that, the Christian's basic premises will be the sanctity of life. Life is God's: he gives it and it is his to take away. A foetus is a baby — a personal individual, a living creature. To call it euphemistically a 'foetus' subtly dehumanises the living being which, in a matter of months, will be a little 'Jane' or 'John' to a mother. Or at the other extreme of age, that old man — 'just a vegetable' to some — matters to God, and it is therefore degrading and offensive to classify him in that kind of way. Senile he may be, and yes, socially useless, but still a child of God. We must repeat, in case of misunderstanding, that the Christian is aware of the problems which give rise to the cries for abortion and euthanasia. Yet he must seek to state positively and with grace the Christian attitude to life, and to sign-post God's loving and staggering care for each human person.

The Church is called into social and political action

God's people are called to live for God in the world; not to withdraw from it but to represent God in his creation. Of course, we need no reminder that the Church is now just a minority group and therefore has a most Herculean struggle to bring meaning into a world which appears to be making a most determined effort to commit suicide. The Constantine era is over. No longer can the Church wield the political and spiritual power that made Valentinian II bow before Bishop Ambrose, or Charlemagne before Pope Leo III. Christians are of no more significance than any other group of people in a world where the big battalions count. This is not a call to despair, but for hope, because instead of propping up the establishment, the Church is free at last to get on with its primary task of transforming individuals and society.

The role of the Christian community in the world appears to be threefold. Firstly, to be the prophetic voice of God. The prophets, it will be recalled, never separated the political and social issues from spiritual matters in their statements concerning the nations. They were prepared to attack spiritual leaders for their neglect of others and for their tacit support of evil (Amos 7:10-17), and also temporal leaders for their neglect of the spiritual dimension (Jer. 26:1-6). Similarly, Christians are called upon to speak discerningly and boldly to society's needs in the light of the revelation through Christ.

Secondly, the Christian community is to be an advocate of those in need. The Church must not serve class interests or its own interests but the interests of others. Spread as it is throughout the world with its professional ministers living on the job, so to speak, it has a unique and wonderful opportunity to speak up on behalf of the deprived, the needy, and the unloved. The gospel is not a social message but the implications of it are social. To ignore the practical implications of the gospel is to debase it. 'People who insist on keeping their hands clean are likely to find themselves without hands,' was Charles Péguy's memorable epigram about political involvement; similarly, Christians who keep themselves aloof from the needs of the world should not be too surprised if they are ignored. They must follow their Lord who believed in getting into human situations and not retiring from them. F. R. Barry wrote: 'The Church is in the world — not in the sacristy or in a vacuum — and it is in the world to redeem it.'[15]

Lastly, the Christian community is called to be an initiator of change. The Church hasn't had a good record in recent years, we must acknowledge. We can point proudly to people like Wilberforce, Shaftsbury, Dr. Barnardo and others, but they lived a long time ago and the modern Church, generally speaking, has not shared their social or humanitarian concerns. Of course, there are wonderful exceptions to this, such as Martin Luther King and Bishop Muzorewa, but, by and large, the indictment is justified — the Church has failed to take seriously its impressive doctrine of the uniqueness of the individual. Nevertheless, whatever the reasons for this neglect, the role of the Christian community is to live out the gospel of the Kingdom, which is for all Christians the model of a Church and also the symbol of hope in a world which although dark is still God's world.

NOTES

1   Read, *Rethink* by G. R. Taylor (Secker and Warburg, 1972), p. 140.
2   J. Jeremias, *The Central Meaning of the New Testament* (SCM, 1965), p. 16.
3   J. Jeremias, *op. cit.*, p. 21.
4   Charles Mayer, *Man faces his Destiny* (Johnson, 1968), p. 133.
5   B. F. Skinner, *Beyond Freedom and Dignity* (Cape, 1972).
6   René Dubos, *So Human an Animal* (Scribner, 1968).
7   L. Feuerbach, *The Essence of Christianity* (Harper Torchbooks, 1957), p. 184.
8   L. Paul, *Alternatives to Christian Belief* (Hodder and Stoughton, 1970), p. 68.
9   J. P. Sartre, *Existentialism and Humanism* (Methuen, 1948), p. 33.
10   J. P. Sartre, *Being and Nothingness* (Washington Square Press, 1966), p. 784.
11   A. Camus, *The Rebel.*
12   F. Tönnies, *Community and Society* (1887; E. T. 1955).
13   Tertullian, *Apology*, XXIX.
14   Ed. S. Benko and J. O'Rourke, *Early Church History* (Oliphants, 1971), p. 113.
15   F. R. Barry, *Recovery of Man* (Religious Book Club, 1948), p. 5. For further exploration of this theme see *Culture against Man* by Jules Henry (Penguin Books, 1972).

CHAPTER 7

Male and Female He Created Them

MAN IS A sexual being. An unoriginal statement, yes, but one that is strangely ignored by most books on the nature of man. While they deal very thoroughly with his depravity, rationality and other aspects of his nature, the sexual basis of his life is commonly disregarded. This omission is surprising for two reasons, natural and theological.

First of all, nature informs us in no uncertain fashion of the centrality of sex. The colours and perfumes of flowers, the plumage and song of birds, animal instincts, human habits and behaviour, our customs and occupations, beauty and charm — in all these things and more sex is never absent. No matter how sophisticated human society may be, however rational its structures, it can never escape the fact that sex pervades human existence.

This fact also emerges most clearly in the Bible. Animal creation is told to 'be fruitful and multiply' (Gen. 1:22) and this command is extended to man but with significant and profound difference — here sex is placed in the context of a relationship with another. In both Genesis 1 and 2, two slightly different accounts of creation, there is described the dual and complementary sides of humanity. Genesis 1:27 narrates that 'God created Man (*Adam*) in his own image, in the image of God he created *him*, male (*Zakar*) and female (*Negebhah*) he created them.' Man is created as a bi-sexual species, in which male and female stand equally together because they are created together. The same point is made in Genesis 2 although with some important differences. In this account the loneliness of Adam is stressed; he is cut off from the animal world because he is in a special relationship to God. Yet, at the same time, he is isolated from God because he does not share God's nature. 'It is not good that man should be alone' (v. 18), sums up a fact we all know well enough, that we are made for fellowship with others. And this fellowship is realised in its most intimate form in a sexual relationship. Adam is, therefore, given a 'helpmeet', symbolically taken from his side, that is, out of his nature. Neither he, nor creation, is completed until woman takes her place alongside man.

While the terminology of Chapter 2 is not as clear as we would like, we can see in it hints of man's dual nature. For example, notice the curious ambiguity between *Adam*, the name for the species, and *ish*, the name for the male of the species. Thus woman (*ishah*) is made from man, *Adam* (v. 22) and is brought to the man (*Adam*) who says 'she shall be called woman because she was taken out of man (*ish*)'. Whatever the reasons for the assimilation between *Adam* and *ish* we can be confident that the passage agrees with Genesis 1 in viewing humanity as dual in being and destiny.

Genesis 1 Adam — male (*Zakar*) and female (*Negebhah*)

Genesis 2 Adam — man (*ish*) and woman (*ishah*)

In these passages, then, two immense ideas interrelate with each other and affect one another, that man is a sexual being and this sexuality is God-given, and that male and female are made for each other and are only complete by belonging together.

It is apparent, therefore, that the starting point for both Judaism and Christianity is the firm relationship between man's sexuality and the role and status of woman. She is not created as an inferior creature but a person with dignity and of equal standing before God. So Brunner writes, 'God created man in his own image and created him as man and woman.'[1] It is in this intimacy of relationship that sexuality is set in the Bible. So close indeed is the connection between sexuality and the position of woman, that to dehumanise women inevitably distorts the relationship between men and women; and the trivialisation of sex leads inexorably to a division between the sexes.

BONDAGE AND FREEDOM

Indictment against Christianity

Yet, in spite of this creative and very rich basis whereby woman is given a theological and theoretical equality and common destiny with man, Christianity has often been accused of retarding the full emancipation of women and of desexualising human life.

There is truth in this accusation. In spite of Christianity's real contribution to the protection of the family unit, the Church has acted timidly concerning the rights of women and the place of sex in human experience.

Why is this? The reasons are both sociological and theological. It is often forgotten that Christianity in the early centuries had to combat the most appalling sexual licence which degraded man and denigrated woman. The Church met such permissiveness, which it saw as a denial of the humanity of man, with a legalism based upon a suspicion of sex and a distrust of human ability to treat it with respect and honour. Yet there can be no doubt that the contrast between Church and society was quite staggering for people who lived at that time. The Church was the place where purity reigned, where relationships were honoured, where women were given an honourable and respected place. We may regret that early Christianity did not liberate women further, but at least within the Church they were treated with dignity.[2]

But the most important causes which restricted the position of women were theological, or to be strictly accurate, distortions of Christian theology. For example, the enticing allures of Eve were seen as the gateway for evil to attack an unsuspecting and well-meaning Adam. Tertullian addresses women in this way, urging upon them modesty of dress and behaviour: 'Do you not know that you are (each) an Eve? The sentence of God on this sex of yours lives in this age...you are the Devil's gateway, you are the unsealer of that forbidden tree, you are the first deserters of the divine law; you are she who persuaded him whom the devil was not valiant enough to attack. You destroyed so easily God's image, man'.[3] In

short, woman is a symbol of temptation, a perpetual reminder of man's fall, and a source of danger to his spiritual life.
'The glance of a woman,' a fourth-century monk wrote, 'is a
poisoned dart.'[4]

False ideas of salvation also began to lend a hand. The
common failure of the Church to appreciate fully the New
Testament doctrine of grace, replacing it instead by an
emphasis upon man's deeds and meritorious works inevitably
led to a lop-sided estimate of the importance of sexual
morality. Sexual sins were among those most to be avoided,
and celibacy received the greatest commendation. It was said
of Ambrose of Milan, who had immense influence upon
Augustine of Hippo, that he was never tired of preaching
virginity, so much so that mothers tried to stop their
daughters attending his church! Comparing marriage to
life-long virginity he preached, 'I consider one thing necessary, I admire another.'

Scriptural backing for the second-class nature of women
was not hard to discover. Appeal was made to those parts of
the New Testament where submission is taught as the social
and spiritual duty of Christian women. Paul's attitude to
women was especially admired and commended. His prefer-
ence for celibacy in 1 Cor. 7 became the model for the
spiritual person, but the context of that chapter in the
expectation of the imminent coming of the Lord was ignored.

It was in fact in the context of her sexuality that early
Christians understood womanhood. As a sexual being she was
feared because of her power over man; as a wife and mother
she was tolerated and contained; as a virgin (de-sexed, so to
speak) she was venerated.

Steady emancipation

Since the beginning of this century we have witnessed the
steady emancipation of women. One by one traditionally-
accepted bastions of male privilege have conceded, sometimes
very reluctantly, to pressure from within society and women
allowed within hallowed courts of male chauvinism. There
can be little doubt that the effects of women's liberation will
be amongst the most significant sociological trends of the

twentieth century. Yet, we should note, whilst we do not despise the considerable contribution of the suffragettes and other reformers, the reasons for this change of attitude are due more to natural, cultural and scientific developments than protests from women themselves. Universal education has given them new confidence and awareness of their equality with men, even in what were once considered purely male provinces. Technology has given the housewife innumerable home gadgets which have taken much of the drudgery out of housework, so creating some release from the bondage of the home. Social pressures for smaller families and better contraceptive methods have also contributed towards making women more independent and more open to society.

Woman, in short, is more free now than she has ever been, but there are signs that the opportunities which are now hers contain elements which, instead of leading to genuine liberty posit the threat of a new and more sinister bondage which masquerades as freedom.

A new bondage?

Freedom is never genuine freedom when it ends in exploitation and the dehumanisation of people. The threat to womanhood comes in two major forms; firstly by the trivialising of sex and, secondly, by the denigration of relationships. Although mankind as a whole is bound to suffer as well by such forces, it is the woman who suffers most keenly because she is both subject and victim in the web of human sexuality and relationships.

Let us take the first threat, the trivialising of sex. We notice that this attitude is the exact opposite of the traditional Christian position which has always treated sex as of the utmost seriousness, even though, as we have seen, it has sometimes treated it negatively. History will no doubt show that to cheapen and trivialise sex is the more evil of the two extremes. The trivialising of the sexual nature of man is seen by the tendency to treat sex either as something basically *simple* or as *play*. On the one hand, sex is viewed as but the release of a gland — the natural, inevitable and therapeutic discharge of a physical need. It is, then, a simple appetite which like hunger needs to be satisfied. It is not surprising that Dr. Alex Comfort's best-selling book *The Joy of Sex* is subtitled a 'Gourmet guide to love making' because it sets out deliberately to show ways how the human appetite for sensuality may be satisfied.[5] But the sexual act is anything but simple, capable as it is of being the centre of endless permutations of perversion, as well as being the heart of the most intimate human love. It may be the simple physical act of two bodies engaging, but there is more to human nature than the desire to copulate. It is often forgotten that promiscuity scars, a fact which most women understand more sensitively than men do. It is significant that in a double review of Comfort's book in the *Sunday Times*, by a man and a woman, it was the woman, Jill Tweedie, who pointed out the dangers of seeing the sexual act as one which has to be satiated by an endless variety of sexual gymnastics. She comments, 'There is, I venture to say, a built-in hazard to majoring in these techniques that may defeat its own ends. There is a very fine line between giving physical pleasure and inflicting mental distress.'[6]

On the other hand, the sexual nature of man is also endangered by treating it merely as *play*. Man, *homo ludens* has perfected play. A glance at any culture will show how important play is. Lack of play will not only make 'Jack a dull boy' it will also indicate how unnatural he is, as well.[7] Man has also converted his sexual urges into play and in so doing has transformed the physical act of sexual intercourse. He has moved it away from the area of instinct, and from its role of propagation of the species, into a pleasurable and meaningful encounter with his partner. Unlike other animals which come together for that brief moment of copulation, the overtures of erotic play which precede orgasm in human intercourse are as important as the climax itself. There is, of course, nothing wrong with physical love, or erotic love when it is the embodiment of a loving relationship. But the sexual act treated only as play between people, and divorced from tender, mature and ongoing relationships leads to making woman a plaything for male enjoyment. Such a hedonistic view of sexuality is expressed most clearly in the philosophy of Hugh Hefner, founder and first apostle of the 'Playboy' empire. The message coming loud and clear from this source is that sex is a commodity to be bought, and women are instruments of pleasure. So the young man, in a *Playboy* cartoon, says to the disarrayed girl he is passionately fondling, 'Why speak of love at a time like this?' Sex, this philosophy proclaims, must be contained within the recreation-entertainment zone; play mustn't become 'serious'.[8] The same approach to sex and to woman is taken in Heller's book *Catch 22*, where one airman estimates a girl as one 'he could make love to instead of falling in love with'.

Sex trivialised either as a simple natural expression or as a game, not only devalues woman, making her the object of indiscriminate masculine desire and fantasy, but also distorts the sexual nature of humanity as a whole. When sexuality becomes a solitary quest for pleasure, man is dehumanised also. Man is more than just an extension of his genital organs, and to live for the next orgasm is quite obviously a less than human way to behave.

But in the current denigration of relationships the status and role of women is also indirectly under attack, because former areas in which the female found most pleasure and fulfilment are being challenged. The family unit, for example, questioned by Edmund Leach in his Reith Lectures, *A Runaway World?* has also been under considerable fire from the leaders of the Women's Liberation Movement. It is pilloried as being 'socially destructive' and an 'obstacle' to feminine freedom. So Germaine Greer in her provocative though sour book, *The Female Eunuch*, encourages women to refuse marriage in order to fight for the right to be women in the world, and shake off 'the chains with which prejudice, religion, and physical force have imprisoned her to marriage and the family'.[9] A more radical cry for 'liberation' for women comes from Miss Firestone's book *The Dialectic of Sex*. She demands the release of women 'from the tyranny of their reproductive biology by every means available, and the diffusion of the childbearing and childrearing role to the society as a whole, men as well as women'.[10] This indeed amounts to an all-out war on the family, challenging the permanence of relationships between husband and wife and

the woman's role as mother. To return to Germaine Greer
once more, 'Women's liberation, if it abolishes the patriarchal
family, will abolish a necessary substructure of the authoritarian state and once that withers away Marx will have come
true willy-nilly, so let's get on with it.'[11] It is clear for both
authoresses, although never explicitly stated, that rejection of
the marriage bond is also a rejection of masculine relationships, even though free sexual relationships are encouraged.
According to Miss Greer the closest and deepest relationships
of the true feminist will be with her 'sisters'.[12]

Here then is the unhappy paradox of modern woman, that
the prospect of full emancipation is threatened by the
presence of elements which by dividing her from men, rob
her of genuine and harmonious development. John Passmore,
commenting on the musical *Hair*, sees expressed in it not
women's liberation but women's bondage.

'Women are mere hangers-on, no longer sexually necessary.
Girls are dressed as boys, rather than, for all their long hair
and decorative garb — boys as girls. The sexual relationships suggested and simulated are not for the most part of a
genital kind; they are anal and oral relationships, for which
women are not necessary. What we are perhaps witnessing
in the name of "community" is a revolt against women,
but a revolt in which women themselves participate
because it can be represented, as by Simone de Beauvoir,
as a revolt against the conception of a "feminine role". It is
Eve, not Adam, who must vanish, if the original state of
perfect humanity is to be regained; she must take her old
place, in Adam's rib, no longer separated flesh. This is not
the first time that a class has participated in a revolution of
which in the end it is the victim.'[13]

Could it be, then, that the militant feminist movement of our
day is not, in fact, a real women's movement at all, but a
form of masculinism which denies true femininity?

In any case, mankind as a whole is impoverished when
women are unable to realise their full potentiality alongside
men, and for that reason it is of the utmost importance that
liberation for women is not divorced from the interests of the

community as a whole. It is precisely at this point that the Biblical teaching concerning the personhood and status of women has so much to teach modern people, because many of the ideals and aspirations of those who call for the full expression of womanhood in the community were already anticipated in the teaching of Jesus and the New Testament. There is much also that clashes sharply with certain contemporary thought which demands our attention as well.

Christian Insight Concerning Womanhood

A true understanding of the radical nature of Christ's teaching about women can only be gained by understanding the plight of a woman in Jewish society. In it the man was supreme and the woman had few rights to call her own. A girl was usually betrothed between the age of twelve and twelve-and-a-half, and the formal marriage took place one year later. With marriage she passed from the power of her father to that of her husband, whom she was obliged to obey as she would a master. The husband was called '*Rab*' (master) and her servile relationship to him was expressed in her duty to prepare his cup, wash his face, hands and feet. Furthermore the security of her home was threatened by the fact that divorce was easy and was almost exclusively the privilege of the husband. If the man were leprous, mentally afflicted, or belonged to a despised trade such as a 'dung collector' the wife could take up divorce proceedings, but the options indicate that she scarcely had any legal rights to speak of.

If the woman's role in the family was scarcely distinguishable from that of a slave, she gained little consolation from a religion that was strictly a masculine affair. She could go no further into the temple than the Court of the Gentiles and the Court of Women. In the synagogue conditions were just as strict; the female section was separated from the rest and women were forbidden to teach or read the Torah — they were there just to listen. Rabbi Eliezer, champion of the traditions, kept Judaism firmly out of the reach of woman and stated that 'it would be better to burn the Torah than to teach it to women'.[14] It is not the least surprising, therefore, that the heartfelt prayer which Jewish men prayed daily was 'Blessed be God that hath not made me a woman.'[15]

1. Spiritual equality

This brief outline of the status of women in Jewish society makes us appreciate the revolutionary character of Jesus's attitude towards the female sex. He moved with easy grace among women and drew some of them into the closest circle of his disciples. That a man should have had such a following among women must have horrified many of his contemporaries. But Jesus was no womaniser, as some have insinuated from the mutual affection between him and women like Mary Magdalene, Mary and Martha. The evidence is clear from the Gospels that his acceptance of women was as full and as free as his acceptance of men. In other words, he saw women as spiritual beings with rights and needs of their own, because they too were created by God and for him.

In two small incidents in Jesus's ministry we can detect the value that he gave to womanhood.

First of all in his attitude to divorce. Against those who by manipulation of the law treated marriage lightly, Jesus reaffirmed its deep sanctity and the obligation it placed upon each partner (Mark 10:2-10). His repetition of the Creation ordinance, that marriage made the partners in the marriage bond 'one flesh', was in itself an implied rebuke to the whole Jewish tradition which, by making woman just a chattel, made marriage less than it should have been. He goes back beyond Deuteronomy 24:1 to the original intention of God whose will it was that man and woman should be joined together in an indissoluble union (Gen. 2:24). In so doing Jesus raised woman to a new level of significance; no longer a piece of property, she was now a partner as God had always intended her to be (Mark 10:11).

Secondly, we note Jesus's estimate of women in his reply to the Sadducees about marriage in heaven (Mark 12:18-27). They set him a trick question based upon Jewish law. The law dictated that if a man died without children his nearest male relative should marry the widow to raise up children to perpetuate his brother's name. The curious conundrum set before Jesus was this: If there were seven brothers, each of whom, having married the same girl, died without issue, whose wife would she be at the resurrection? The assumption that the role and status of woman in heaven are but extensions of her earthly lot could scarcely be called a good advertisement for heaven for a Jewish girl! Jesus's reply, so simple, expresses the heart of Christian humanity. 'You are mistaken. When they rise from the dead, men and women do not marry, they are like angels in heaven.' Woman is placed with dignity beside man as part of God's intended and eternal plan. In Christ's view she is not a piece of property which could be passed on from man to man, but a person of value in the sight of her Maker. How startling and original this concept must have seemed.

Paul — 'A male chauvinist pig'?

According to many supporters of equality for women St. Paul is the *bête noire* of the Christian tradition. In the opinion of one English undergraduate, Paul was a 'male chauvinist pig'! Was he? No; such a view is a false and superficial judgment on a man who brought very profound insights to bear upon the status of women. Yet at the same time we acknowledge that his theology contains traditional as well as radical elements and these blend uneasily in his writings.

Let us begin with the more radical side of his teaching. First of all, he continued his Lord's high opinion of the spiritual equality of women, and showed that in Christ the man-made barriers between classes, nations, and the sexes are completely done away; 'there is neither male nor female, but all are one in Christ Jesus' (Gal. 3:28). Here is the charter of woman's liberty in Christ; in Christ there is now no spiritual distinction between men and women, but both are united and equal in him. From what we know of the New Testament Church this equality in Christ found its practical outlet in the contribution of women's gifts within the community. They devoted themselves to works of charity (Acts 9:36); showed hospitality (Acts 16:14 ff.); laboured in the task of evangelism (Rom. 16:1, 6); imparted instruction (Acts 18:26); shared in the Pentecostal gift (Acts 2:1 ff.); and charismatic gifts were not denied them (Acts 21:9; 1 Cor. 11:5).

Secondly, Paul displays a high ideal of marriage which is illustrated by the way he uses it as a model of the relationship between Christ and the Church. No one who had a low concept of the relationships between husband and wife could have possibly used it to describe the love between the Lord and his people. The Church-wife comparison which Paul uses, to show the loving relationship between Christ and his Church, by implication suggests that for Paul the marriage bond was one where the female had an honourable, respected and dignified status.

Finally, we must note Paul's unique contribution to the understanding of sexuality. Not for him was sex just an 'appropriate exercise of the genital organs', to use Sherwin Bailey's phrase.[16] In his teaching concerning prostitution at Corinth Paul enunciated the principal of the psychosomatic unity expressed in sexual intercourse. 'Do you not know that he who joins himself to a prostitute becomes one body with her? For it is written "the two shall become one"' (1 Cor. 6:16). Sexual intercourse is seen by him as an act between a man and his wife so intimate that the fusing of the bodies is a sign of a deeper unity between personality and spirit. Given this 'sacramental' relationship we may see that for Paul intercourse is a precious and spiritual symbol which attacks all trivialising tendencies. Sexual activity implies a deep, personal and permanent relationship.

To what appears to be a profound and imaginative extension of the revolutionary views of Jesus concerning relationships between the sexes, Paul also contributes elements which seem tame and traditional in comparison. Concerning relationships, he urges wives to be submissive to their husbands (Eph. 5:21) and to be obedient and meek (1 Tim. 1:9-12). The basis for such subjection is taken from a number of different comparisons. In 1 Cor. 11, the Father's lordship over Christ supplies the basis, whereas in Eph. 5 the subordination of the Church to Christ is viewed as the model for the obedience of wives to husbands. In 1 Tim. 2, however, appeal is made to the Creation as showing, without doubt, the priority of men. Concerning the role of women, certain passages occur which appear to restrict the exercise of women's gifts in the Church. They are expected to keep silence in the Church and they are forbidden to teach (1 Cor. 14:34; 1 Tim. 2:12). Such injunctions clash most oddly with the outpouring of God's Spirit upon all flesh, Paul's expectation that all gifts should be used responsibly and freely (1 Cor. 12:4-13), and most of all with his recognition of women prophetesses (1 Cor. 11:1-15).

These two remarkably opposing tendencies in Paul's thinking are not easily reconcilable. We do not know, for example, the social thinking of the time nor the particular problems of the Church set in the Roman world of the first century. A 'go-slow' policy may have been necessary because of the nature of Paul's society. There are indications, however, in some of Paul's more traditional teaching that he was conscious that they clashed with the gospel he preached. Thus in his argument for the superiority of man in 1 Corinthians 11 he asserts that 'woman was made for man' (v. 8). Yet he is clearly unhappy about the result of this argument and adds in parenthesis, 'nevertheless in the Lord woman is not independent of man, nor man of woman, for as woman was made from man, so man is now born of woman. And all things are from God' (v. 11). This conclusion weakens his argument because what was intended to prove the submission of women to men, concludes as a statement of mutual interdependence!

Or take Ephesians 5 where women are instructed to be subject to the husband who is the head. As in 1 Corinthians 11 the husband represents Christ in the analogy, but now a remarkable *volte face* occurs. The hierarchical argument of 1 Corinthians 11 — God, Christ, man, woman — is replaced by those virtues which govern relationships; love, honour and obedience. If Christ represents the role of husband it is clear this his lordship is displayed not by dominion but by service; 'Husbands, love your wives, as Christ loved the Church and gave himself up for her.' As Brunner expresses it, 'the function of leadership does not denote masterfulness of *dominium* but a *ministerium*.[17] What has happened? Could it be that Paul's teaching about the submission of women stemmed more from the established custom of his day, and this has been innocently, though awkwardly, joined to the radical gospel of Christ in which love is central? Christ rules by love and in this environment of love he only rules by personal freedom and responsibility. Such instructions as 'obey', 'submit', 'be quiet' and so on when applied only to the wife do not emerge from the essence of the gospel but reflect, we are bold to suggest, the social duties of first-century Jewish-Hellenistic culture in which Christianity was set. Indeed, we must add, obedience, love, sacrifice, belong to the structure of *all* Christian relationships, not only that of marriage, and apply equally to men and women and we cannot simply compartmentalise them. As Pannenberg remarks, 'Christian love implies the liberation of fellow men to freedom and equality.'[18] If Christ is the model for manhood, (and he cannot be that exclusively), then it is a model in which service and humility are uppermost virtues and in which masculine arrogance finds no place.

Thus we see that spiritual equality has consequences reaching far beyond the purely spiritual realm. The gospel which makes women equal to men in Christ, and black men equal to white men through the gospel, cannot be restricted to the spiritual dimension. Just as the slave Onesimus is now a brother in status and name to his former owner (Philem. vv. 10, 17) so equality cannot stop short of social relationships. But we must recognise, frankly, that equality is a mischievous will-of-the-wisp, an impossible Utopia, unrealisable because of differences in intellectual ability, environment, culture and opportunity. The Christian interpretation of equality must insist not on the questionable claim of equality of talents but on equality of rights. The gospel teaching that God loves all, must equally have as its corollary that each individual person should be able to live in such freedom that his or her potential as man or woman may develop without restriction. The shame of traditional Christianity has been a failure to understand fully the implications of Christ's teaching about womanhood. It has accepted too readily the customs of the socio-cultural systems in which it has been set, and has not shown forth in its own life the model of true liberation.

2. The complementarity of the sexes

By complementarity is meant the function of relationships wherein the self is fulfilled or completed in the other. We can take obvious examples from ordinary life. A man needs a wife for him to be a husband; a woman needs a child to be a mother; and the growing child confers on his parents a blessing by fulfilling them in their role as parents. In each case it is not just a name that is given but a new understanding of the self as one gives to the other. Complementarity is not inequality but fulfilment in relation to another. We know from human relationships that it is most difficult to separate the 'I' from others. The person I think I am cannot easily be abstracted from the person others tell me I am, or myself in the multiplicity of roles I play in society. We need others to find and know ourselves, and without others we are incomplete.

This is also true between the sexes. In this case complementarity signifies that true humanity is only achieved when both sexes achieve maturity, existing in full interdependence with each other. There are, however, two issues of importance which affect the concept of complementarity. The first is a basic one of identity; is it true that there is a *difference* of kind between the humanity of man and that of woman? Or is it that such differences, apart from the obvious physical differences, are merely the result of cultural conditioning? The second issue is a practical question of relationships; if there are far reaching differences between the sexes, what is the *significance* of this for human society?

Difference

The Bible does not speculate about the nature of woman although there is the implicit assumption throughout that statements concerning the physical and spiritual constitution of the male apply equally to the female. She also is 'flesh', a 'living soul', and open to God's Spirit. But the Bible also indicates that there is a unique, deep and fundamental difference between male and female which is as old as humanity itself. The account in Genesis, whether taken as a special creation or as an expression of the emergence of mankind from the womb of a natural evolutionary process, makes woman an integral part of man but does not confuse her with the masculine element. Woman is made for man and man for woman. The implications not just sexual. As 'helpmeet' she is his fellow, companion as well as wife and lover. She complements him as he does her.

This understanding of woman clashes sharply with popular views, especially the opinions of leaders of the Women's Liberation Movement. Germaine Greer, Julie Mitchells and others see the argument from difference as a conspiracy against women. They contend that there are no innate differences between the character traits or abilities of men and women. Germaine Greer, for example, points out that the genetic difference between the sexes amounts to the fact that of the forty-eight chromosomes in the human cell only one is peculiar to the masculine nature. She agrees that Frenchmen may say *vive la différence* but pours withering scorn on the assumption of man that women are completely different; 'on this difference we base a complete separation of male and female, pretending as it were that all forty-eight were different'.[19] In her view women have been hoodwinked into believing they are the weaker, junior, less intelligent sex. Simone de Beauvoir echoes this opinion: 'one is not born, but rather becomes a woman,' she states, arguing that social pressures mould the girl into a feminine ideal.[20]

As anthropologists point out, many of the traits associated with masculine and feminine natures vary from culture to culture. In one tribe the female may hunt and take an aggressive role whilst the male remains at home to protect the children. In another tribe, where procreation is highly valued, men may participate very fully in the care and nurture of children from birth to puberty. In Western society masculine/feminine roles have altered considerably over the last decade or so. Men are more closely involved in the life of the home and share in activities which only a comparatively short time ago would have been considered exclusive feminine pursuits. It is no longer remarkable if a man remains behind at home to look after the children while the woman becomes the bread-winner.

While there is considerable variety in the way that different societies have defined the roles of men and women, we suggest that the Biblical teaching of a fundamental difference between the humanities of man and woman is basically correct. It is the unique contribution of Margaret Mead's book *Male and Female*[21] that instead of asking the usual question, 'Are the differences between male and female due to heredity or culture?' she prefers to ask, 'Are there basic similarities in the ways in which men and women in every society have experienced being male or female?' She replies in the affirmative. These similarities, in her opinion, stem from the biological nature of the sexes and their respective encounters with their environment. Examining the different roles of male and female in the family group, she draws attention to the passive relationship to nature on the part of the female, whereas the male's relationship is more active and self-differentiating. These differences are seen from birth. In every society the person closest to the child is the mother. Both boy and girl obviously must find their own distinct individualities apart from the mother, but their experience of this distinction from the parent is very different. The little girl already has a model of motherhood in her own mother and she learns that she will attain womanhood merely by waiting. Her history as a female is punctuated by the inevitable progress of bodily events and bodily alterations: menstruation, pregnancy, childbirth, menopause. She has no need to prove herself a woman. Her body tells her this clearly enough. But masculine experience is not the same. To be a man is to be unlike the closest person to him; instead of imitating, he must break with that original identification with his mother.

For the boy manhood is not merely a matter of bodily maturation, because of course he has nothing like the physical changes of the woman to convince him of his maturity. Growing up, therefore, becomes a challenge which he must accept, or remain a child. He cannot wait for fulfilment because it is something he must win, something he must prove to himself. In Valerie Goldstein's view the difference is that 'masculinity is an endless process of becoming, while in feminity, the emphasis is on being.'[22] The male, aggressive, active in his continual struggle with his environment; the female, a more passive being, is in a closer, more intuitive relationship with her environment and responds to it more instinctively and perhaps more naturally.[23]

This conclusion arrived at by anthropological studies is supported by recent research in genetics. The evidence now accumulating from several quarters strongly rejects the notion that sexual differences stop at the neck! Man is not psycho-sexually neutral at birth; rather, we are informed, the organisation of the central nervous system during pre-natal development predisposes the infant at birth to masculine or feminine response and behaviour. This means that the new-born baby is not a clean slate on which society may inscribe its will, but a slate on which has already been written its response as a male or female human being.

If this is so, the differences between men and women should not be ignored, obliterated, or ridiculed, but accepted as integral and complementary elements of human exper-ience. Women are not to be seen as junior males, or as 'defective males', as Aristotle believed, but as women with a woman's viewpoint, and with a distinctive way of looking at reality which is in no way inferior to the masculine interpre-tation, but different. Difference is an essential part of complementarity and it is by acceptance of difference that genuine wholeness takes place.

This is the Christian vision: that sameness and difference between the sexes implies not an equality which must be fought for at all costs, but a complementarity which must be sought, in which male and female may grow together in harmony and mutual respect.

Significance

Equality of right and opportunity implies that womanhood must be allowed to develop freely, and the gifts given allowed full expression. If we feel that this should apply in society it should also relate to the Church. If God has given gifts to his people — to men and women — they should and must be exercised within the community and for the benefit of all. Church, society and home provide the contexts in which men and women must work together to bring out the best in themselves and in one another. This will only happen if fear, prejudice and distrust are replaced by love and confidence. It is salutary to remember that in Paul's great discourse on the uses and abuses of spiritual gifts he makes the point that God's gifts, given to all, were not given to demonstrate superiority over one another or for self-edification but to build up the body of Christ. Women, similarly, within the Church must have adequate opportunity to use their gifts for the well-being of the Church as a whole. This conclusion, that women must be allowed to exercise their God-given gifts in the congregation, is very relevant to our churches today. There are no really sound theological reasons why women should not be full ministers or priests in the Christian Church. It is a scandal that many Christian bodies should still oppose this. Women's ministry is generally put in a second-class category, although nobody ever describes it as such. We should not be too surprised if gifted women do not consider full-time Christian service at the moment as a worthwhile option. Prejudice, ignorance, intolerance and indifference must face up to the fact that *womankind is humankind.*

But equality of opportunity must not be confused with equality of function. Men and women are human beings but not identical beings. The two sexes have received a different stamp, and whilst both are called to live as persons they will live in different ways because their experience of life is different. Man's experience of life as a man, and a woman's experience as a woman, necessarily means that the one is excluded from a range of human experience which belongs to the other. A woman's role and function in a society will normally be limited by her nature as a woman, however talented and able she may be. Free though she may be to choose what to do with her life, she will normally feel the call of her nature to be a wife and mother. Contrary to feminist writing, marriage and motherhood are areas of great satisfaction for many intelligent and professional women. Instead of interfering with their lives, there is evidence that as wives and mothers women find fulfilment in these roles.[24]

In the New Testament the role of women in the home is

taken very seriously. They are reminded frequently of the great opportunity they have within the family unit to show the love of God in their lives and behaviour. To be a wife and mother is not second best if the love-relationship between man and wife is constant, and if the real sense of complementarity is maintained. It is only second best if that home becomes a barrier shutting off the girl from realising her genuine humanity. Ibsen portrayed this problem beautifully in his play, *A Doll's House*. Nora asks Helmer, 'What do you consider is my most sacred duty?' 'Your duty,' Helmer replies 'is to your husband and children.' Nora however hesitates and replies, 'I have another duty, just as sacred, a duty to myself. I believe that before everything else I'm a human being — just as you are, or at any rate I shall try to become one.'[25] The Christian sympathises with this point of view, but adds that the discovery of one's humanity cannot be done in isolation from one's partner but only with him. This is at the heart of Paul's statement: 'There is neither male nor female, but you are all one in Christ Jesus' (Gal. 3:24). He does not say we are equal in Christ, but *one*; that is, the disruption created by sin has been removed and in Christ the way is opened for a fuller and richer fellowship than has been experienced before — a fellowship now realisable in Christ.

The integration of the sexes involves two important corollaries that bear on the Christian doctrine of man. The first is the observation that in Christian teaching on the subject of humanity, the model has invariably been the model of masculine humanity. From our study of man as both male and female we suggest that many of the insights into the wholeness of human experience have been lost because the profile of human need has been totally masculine in character. A woman's needs, drives and feelings of inadequacy are divergent from masculine experience. Her nature as a woman gives her very sinfulness a different stamp and character. She will respond to a different set of challenges and appeals — those which echo the nature of the feminine.

The second corollary is that Christianity has followed Judaism in framing our concept of God in masculine terms — Father, Son and so on. Of course, such language is analogical. To think otherwise is to create a total barrier between man and woman, and between God and woman. As 'man' is made in God's image, God must be understood as including in himself the vast range of attributes and characteristics which he has given to male and female. Perhaps we need to discover the 'feminine' element of God which comes out frequently in scripture — in his compassion shown to Israel, his passionate love displayed through Hosea, and indeed, we suggest, in the tenderness and love of Jesus so clearly shown in his ministry. It may be in fact that resulting from the full integration of men and women at every level of human experience, we shall be open to understand more closely the nature of God who has given us in human nature certain insights into his own.

3. Love as the clue to the nature of humanity

It is the concept of love so strongly stressed by Jesus which humanises woman and man, and reunites them in a closer and more lasting unity. Love, claimed Jesus, is the absolute and explicit summary of the Law itself, whereby one stands in a relationship of love to God and to one's fellow men. What Jesus preached he also practised, and so showed forth not only what God is like but also how human beings should live.

Love reaches its highest expression, therefore, in a personal relationship in which the one lives on in the life of the other. St. Augustine pointed out that this is true of God himself, who, in his trinitarian nature exemplifies the mysterious relationship of love.[26] It is true of human relationships as well. Without love, relationships are incomplete and fall short of their full potential. Without love, people are not properly recognised as persons; they become, at best, individuals inferior to us — at worst, objects which may be used.

Because of the Biblical teaching that God always sees humanity as persons in need of his love, Christian teaching down the centuries has set sexuality in terms of lasting relationships. Sex is not merely a thing which people do, but is a tangible and personal expression of what they are. Without love, sexual intercourse becomes an end in itself and is sought for its own sake, instead of being an expression of love between two people. Such an idea may seem quaint in a world where permissiveness reigns; where television, plays, books and films overtly assume that premarital sex, extramarital sex, sexual deviations and other forms of promiscuity are acceptable forms of human behaviour. Surely it is old-fashioned and oh, so narrow, to think of sex in terms of abiding relationships? There is a deal of current reaction to indicate that such licence in sexual matters does not meet with the approval or even reflect the morality of the majority of people today. But even if promiscuous relations became the norm in society, the firm teaching of the Bible and the Christian tradition would give the Church the backing to say firmly and authoritatively that sexual intercourse finds its meaning and goal in the love between two human beings in an enduring relationship. Once it is recognised that God is love, and that he created men and women in his image as persons-made-for-love, marriage falls into its natural place as the sphere where human love is experienced at its highest and deepest.

The paradox, however, is that marriage as the nexus of physical love and enduring relationship is significant and important only because it is not the most important thing. That most important thing is one's duty and loyalty to God. The radical teaching of Jesus was that men should put God before all else — even before their families, professions and their own personal lives. This was also at the heart of Paul's teaching. Relationship to God is basic to all other relationships. This does not imperil human relationships by destroying them or weakening them. On the contrary, by coming *in between*, Christ makes them stronger because he now is the uniting factor. Through him men and women come closer together.

The necessity for God at the centre of human sexual relationships is that here may be seen and felt so clearly the tragedy and pain of man's fall. Is there a deeper source of conflict between human beings than sex? Freud once remarked that sex is one of the greatest forces of distingegration. This is so well illustrated in human experience that expansion of this point is not required. If that is so, it is clear that human beings, alone, cannot sustain relationships so demanding and threatening, without the constant nourishment of love from a source beyond themselves. This is where the priority of God in relationships is so important. Love given first to God is always distributed through him to others.

4. Gospel and Law

The Church, like its Lord, is in the 'relationship business'. Its task is to create an environment of love in which men and women live in harmony and trust. Yet the moment we ask how this may be done we encounter all kinds of problems, not least the problem of legalism. If there is one area where Christianity finds it most difficult to resist legalism it is surely in the sphere of sexual relations. Churches which have showed great apathy about social issues can suddenly demonstrate great fervour and unity in a common protest over some moral problem. So Ernst Bloch castigates the Christian Church: 'It bristles at see-through blouses, but not at slums in which half-naked children starve and not above all at the conditions that keep three quarters of mankind in misery. It condemns desperate girls who abort a foetus, but it consecrates war which aborts millions.'[27]

This warning for balance must be heeded, but it is obvious that in matters of human sexuality the Christian is placed between the demands of both gospel and law. The gospel calls him to a freedom which is based upon and contained by Jesus his Lord. No longer under law he is under the law of Christ which is the law of love. 'The gospel is addressed to persons, the law sees acts,' declared Harvey Cox.[28] This finds support in the case of the woman taken in adultery (John 8:1-12). There is no question of her guilt; she stands condemned. Yet Jesus challenges the legalists about to stone her, 'Let him who is without sin among you be the first to throw a stone at her.' In saying this, he turns the law against them too. Jesus, alone with the woman, asks, 'Has no one condemned you? Neither do I, go and sin no more.' Yet while Jesus rejects legalism because it is concerned with acts and ignores the person, he does not replace it with a wishy-washy system of situation ethics. In his reply to the woman forgiveness is inseparable from command. The law looks back, it is not immediately interested in the future. The gospel however not only looks back and utters the word of forgiveness but it looks forward and outlines the true pattern of living. 'Go and sin no more' takes us into the area of *law* because the gospel, which calls the Christian to speak about a new way of life also commits him to exposing the false alternatives to it.

Set, therefore, between gospel and law, the church and Christian are involved in a twofold responsibility.

Negatively, in the sphere of *law*, the Church is called to defend the area of sexuality as a fully human activity and must resist forces which seek to dehumanise it or debase womanhood. The Christian cannot sit back and let family life be destroyed, or remain indifferent to the exploitation of sex. The gospel calls him to defend and protect the innocent, to stand up for justice, purity and morality. The tables of 'money changers' must occasionally be overturned.

But it is of little use to merely recite that extramarital sex is wrong, that promiscuity is wrong, sexual deviancy is wrong and group marriages are wrong — 'because the Bible says so'. Not only is this attitude hopelessly naïve, but it often ends up by depersonalising human sexual relationships by making them dependent upon a supposed divine law. The Church must state logically why they are wrong, why faithfulness in marriage and purity of life are necessary forms of behaviour. For example, we may say that homosexuality is a deviation from God's purposes for mankind, but little good comes from merely describing it as 'wrong' or 'sinful'. This attitude has sometimes caused distress to sensitive homosexuals who cannot understand the basis of such condemnation. It seems to them further proof of Christian intolerance or ignorance. Heterosexuality, like good health, may be God's norm for humanity, but if homosexuality is the result of genetic deformation it is as foolish to condemn the homosexual as a sinner, as it is to upbraid the sick man for being unhealthy! In saying this, we are not trying to relax Christian standards but suggesting that when they are upheld they must be expressed clearly, intelligently and with compassion.[29]

Positively, the gospel proclaims the fact of liberation. Although we cannot 'lay down the law' regardless of the human situation, we can say clearly that Christ can liberate people from the worship of Aphrodite, the worship and bondage of false sexuality, and make their lives clean and strong. Of course we know that, generally speaking, people do not want to be like that! It is the warped nature of our world to laugh at purity and to admire promiscuity: to be pure is to be sexless, is the common deduction. But against such mistaken views the Church must repeat that Christ does not make people eunuchs or destroy them as sexual beings. Rather he straightens them out as people, correcting and guiding their human desires.

Realism demands that we ask, set as we are in pluralist societies, how on earth can we expect the world to listen to and hear the voice of the Church? One small voice among the strident cries of alternative philosophies; there is no compelling reason why the world should listen to us rather than to others. There is only one answer — action. The Christian Church must live the gospel it preaches and show the model of community in which people, men and women, are honoured because they are persons made by God, and made for freedom and respect. It is only on the basis of example that the Church has any right to speak, and it must first set its own house in order if its message is to have any compelling quality. Christian relationships will only seem a genuine alternative to the Women's Lib when it is seen that within the Christian family there is real freedom for women to exercise full and genuine lives alongside men in mutual trust and respect.

NOTES

1 *Man in Revolt*, p. 346.
2 See, *The Man-Woman Relation in Christian Thought*, D. Sherwin Bailey (Longmans, 1959).
3 *On the Apparel of Women*, ch. 1.
4 But, as the confessions of St. Jerome indicate, withdrawal into the desert did not solve the problem of temptation. He admits that he 'sat alone in the company of scorpions and wild beasts and yet was in the company of dancing girls' (*Epistle*, 22).
5 Published by *Quartet Books*, 1974.
6 *The Sunday Times*, March 31st, 1974.
7 An important book on the nature of human play is *Homo Ludens: A Study of the Play Element in Culture* (Routledge and Kegan Paul, 1950).

8   'Playboy and its less successful imitators are not "sex magazines" at all. They are basically anti-sexual. They dilute and dissipate authentic sexuality by reducing it to an accessory but keeping it at a safe distance.' Harvey Cox, The Secular City (SCM, 1966), p. 204.

9   The Female Eunuch (Macgibbon and Kee, 1970).

10 Shulamith Firestone, The Dialectic of Sex (Cape, 1971), p. 33ff.

11 Op. cit., p. 329.

12 The Female Eunuch, p. 19-20 and p. 329.

13 J. Passmore, The Perfectibility of Man (Duckworth, 1970), p. 314. On the commercial exploitation of women's sexuality read Culture Against Man by Jules Henry (Penguin, 1972), pp. 76-86.

14 Jerusalem Talmud, Sotah 3.4.

15 The Mishnah, T. Berakhoth 7.18.

16 In The Man-Woman Relation in Christian Thought.

17 Man in Revolt, p. 359, n. 1.

18 W. Pannenberg, Theology and the Kingdom of God.

19 The Female Eunuch, p. 29.

20 The Second Sex (Cape, reprint 1968), p. 41.

21 Margaret Mead, Male and Female (Pelican reprint, 1975).

22 Valerie Goldstein. 'The human situation; a feminine viewpoint' in, The Nature of Man (Ed., S. Doniger).

23 See also, E. Brunner, Man in Revolt, p. 352ff for an interesting discussion of the differences between the sexes.

24 See, Family Issues of Employed Women in Europe and America, Ed. A. Michel (Brill, Leiden, 1971).

25 Act III.

26 De Trinitate, Book VII, 10.

27 Frontispiece of Man on His Own (Herder, N.Y., 1970).

28 The Secular City, p. 212.

29 We must distinguish between homosexual nature and its expression. The Bible, after all, is quite emphatic that homosexual acts are wrong (Lev. 18:22; 1 Kings 14:24; Rom. 1:25) just as extra-marital heterosexual acts are wrong. We may not be responsible for the tendencies within us, but we are for the way they are expressed.

CHAPTER 8

The Destiny of Man

'ONE OF THE great problems of individualism', wrote B. F. Skinner, 'seldom recognised as such, is death — the inescapable fate of the individual, the final assault on freedom and dignity.'[1] The fact of man's mortality is close to the heart of the problem of man and, as such, is never far away from his anxious thought. It is, as Skinner hints, not so much a problem that there is death, but that 'I' die. We may acknowledge death to be an inevitable fact in a physical universe but few can remain indifferent to their own personal death. Death, then, is not something that confronts man at the end of life's journey, but is with him throughout life, affecting his way of looking at reality and challenging the meaning he sees in life. It forces him to ask, 'Has the individual a glorious destiny — or is he, when life is through, crushed like a discarded cigarette-end under the heel of a meaningless universe?'

For modern secular man, death is the end. This appears to him to be a logical though depressing conclusion. After all, he asks, what value can be given to humanity when modern knowledge speaks in no uncertain terms of man's insignificance? When we are told that the light that reaches our telescopes from our nearest galactic neighbour, the Andromeda nebula, has been travelling through space for two million years, we are staggered by the immensity of the universe. When we are told, further, that countless galactic systems make up the universe, our man-centred view of all things is seen to be absurd. Pascal had reason to exclaim, 'the silence of these infinite spaces frightens me'.[2] But that's not all: we saw in the opening chapter that, through the researches of biology and anthropology, the gap between man and other forms of life has narrowed considerably. What right have we got to suppose that man's life has any more meaning, and his destiny any more glory that that of the beasts which perish?

The secularist does not generally face this with any stoic equanimity of mind. The anthropologist, Malinowski, a self-avowed agnostic, describes how he believes God to be the reality which he desperately needs. Quoting Laplace's reply to Napoleon on the relationship between God and astronomy, 'Sire, I have no need of that hypothesis,' Malinowski comments, 'It is the proud answer of a confident atheist, but it does not ring true to the humble agnostic. On the contrary I should say that God is a reality and not a hypothesis and a reality of which I am in the greatest need, though this need I cannot satisfy or fulfil...personally to me and to many like me, nothing really matters except the answer to the burning question "am I going to live, or shall I vanish like a bubble?" What is the aim and the sense and the issue of all this strife and suffering?'[3]

Malinowski's distress is shared by mankind generally. Man may be mortal but death comes into his life as an alien, to drag him protesting and kicking to a fate which, he feels, contradicts his nature. This protest against death can be traced in the world's literature from its earliest times. We find it in the weary voice of the writer of Ecclesiastes who concluded that death makes futile all the activity of men: 'The fate of the sons of men and the fate of beasts is the same; as one dies, so dies the other. They all have the same breath and man has no advantage over the beasts; for all is vanity. All go to one place; all are from the dirt and all turn to dirt again' (3:19-20). It is echoed by ancient Greek philosophers and dramatists, who were acutely conscious of the transitory nature of all things. 'Death is the most terrible of all things,' exclaims Aristotle, 'for it is the end.'[4] Epicurus, while scorning death, admits that 'death is the most terrifying of all ills'.[5] Sophocles, while extolling the glory of man acknowledges that death is his conqueror; 'Of all the great wonders, none is greater than man...only for death can he find no cure.'[6]

Perhaps no ancient philosopher was more painfully conscious of the transitoriness of life than the noble, but sad, Roman Emperor Marcus Aurelius. Death dominated his entire conception of life, choking its joys and pleasures and interpreting its every little detail: 'When we have meat before us and such eatables, we receive the impression that this is the dead body of a fish and this is the dead body of a bird or a pig.'[7]

This same refrain, that death is frightening and too awful to contemplate, has been taken up in the following centuries into our own day. In Samuel Becket's play *Waiting for Godot* the fact of death as a bleak spectre of life is brilliantly pictured in his merging of birth with death. The mother, 'astride of a grave and a difficult birth. Down in the hole, lingeringly, the grave-digger puts on the forceps.' In Becket's interpretation of life there is no meaning, no purpose — death awaits. This illustration reminds one of Heidegger's definition of man as a 'being-towards-death' (*sein zum Töde*); as 'soon as a human being is alive, he is old enough to die.'[8]

God who resurrects

The awfulness of death is no less strongly emphasised in the Bible. No attempt is made by Biblical authors to soften its impact on human life — it is terrifying and even repugnant. No clear or consistent interpretation is given, furthermore, of the presence of death. That man is by nature mortal and therefore subject to death, and that death came into the world through man's sin are two viewpoints expressed in scripture. What is, however, clearly seen by Biblical writers is that death must be interpreted by two greater facts, that God is Lord of all, and that man's relationship to God is life's supreme good.

For the Israelite life was the highest of goods; a long life, a life with assured posterity to carry on one's name, were the best gifts God could give (Gen. 15:15; Judges 8:32; Job 42:17). Life is a blessing, death is a curse (Deut. 30:19). To die 'full of days' is an enviable dream but to die in the midst of life is an untimely end. Death, however, has no independent role. The Israelite just as firmly believed that God is Lord of death as he is of life; it does not operate independently of him but is under his control as much as life is (Ps. 36:8; Ps. 90:3; Ps. 104:29; 1 Sam. 2:6). No one may have life apart from God; it is a gift bestowed by God, the fountain of life.

Life is given for a purpose. This is clearly expressed in the Old Testament. Its aim was for man to enjoy a rich and fulfilled relationship with God. Death's real misery and curse lay in the unnatural way it negated this promise of an abiding relationship with God. If death triumphs over the godly man the value of this relationship is very questionable indeed. Gradually the hope begins to appear in the Old Testament that death cannot have the last word over God's people; God, the Lord of all, can and will intervene in the realm of the dead.

Nothing says more about God's estimate of man than the death and resurrection of Christ. These events say firmly to man at any point in time; 'You need not die; I have redeemed you and conquered death.' The significance is tremendous. Not only, in Christ, is the power of sin annulled but the fear of death is removed. 'There is no fear in love,' announced John, and the love of the cross draws the sting of the devastating fear of death. Yes, the Christian must die too, but he knows that now there is nothing to dread and much to expect. So Pascal wrote, 'Without Jesus death is horrible, but with Jesus it is holy, kind, and the joy of the true believer.'[9]

Not only is fear vanquished, but physical death itself is given notice. For the Christian it no longer holds any terror, since it is now toothless — no longer a tyrant, it has become a gateway. In these triumphant words John Donne signalled the eventual defeat of death:

> Death be not proud, though some have called thee
> Mighty and dreadful, for, thou art not soe,
> For those, whom thou think'st, thou dost overthrow,
> Die not, poore death, nor yet canst thou kill mee.
> ...Why swell'st thou then?
> One short sleepe past, we wake eternally,
> And death shall be no more; death, thou shalt die.

The cross has changed the shape of death. From being the

spectre which blocks the way of life's promise, death becomes
for Christ's people the pathway of life into the presence of
God. Death is now shaped by the love of God in Christ and as
such it is inconceivable that this God will let his people
perish. The ground of this hope is the resurrection of the Lord
— what the cross declares, the empty tomb verifies; Christ is
alive and man may live in him. For the New Testament
writers the expectation of resurrection was in fact more than a
hope — it was a *fait accompli*. Since God had raised Jesus this
was the irrefutable proof that he would raise all his people in
his good time. The decisive battle has been fought and the
final victory is no longer in doubt.

Not everyone accepts that the resurrection actually happened. There are those who, without even considering the
evidence of Jesus's resurrection, conclude that the dead are
not raised and the resurrection is unbelievable. Others are
convinced that 'something' occurred to create the Christian
faith, but they locate this 'something' in the psychological
fantasies of the disciples. The reader is recommended the
volume in this series entitled *I believe in the Resurrection of Jesus*,
by George Ladd, where the subject is handled in greater
depth. All we need say now is that the resurrection was a
unique, unprecedented event, and as such the disciples had
no historical presuppositions that could become the food for
psychological fantasies. The same holds true for the disciples'
spiritual and theological experience. The Gospels make it
plain that the disciples shared a common misunderstanding
of the events in Jerusalem which Jesus predicted and
expected. They were totally unprepared for the cross and
resurrection, and the shock these events caused them robs
subjective theories of their plausibility. The fact no serious
student of the New Testament can deny is that the first
Christians were convinced that Jesus had been raised from
the dead. There is indeed no faith in the New Testament
which does not start from, and rest upon the firm conviction
that the resurrection of Christ is a clear and verifiable fact. So
Pannenberg comments: 'As long as historiography does not
begin with a narrow concept of reality according to which
"dead men do not rise", it is not clear why historiography
should not in principle be able to speak about Jesus's

resurrection as the explanation that is best established of such events as the disciples' experience of his appearance and the discovery of the empty tomb.'[10]

The significance of the resurrection is twofold.

First of all, Christians see the resurrection as part of the total activity of God demonstrating his nature and his love for mankind. Obviously the resurrection on its own proves little — it needs both *explanation* before, and *interpretation* afterwards, if it is to make sense. The *explanation* before must be seen in the loving activity of God towards mankind, in the way he yearns for a deeper unity between himself and his created people. The raising of Jesus then arises out of a background of redemption. Take it away from this purpose and it becomes a rather pointless divine conjuring trick. The *interpretation* of the resurrection comes after the historical fact in the repeating of the resurrection in human experience. The resurrection has important implications for man's future and eternity, but it also has bearings upon human existence now. The Christian life should be lived as an experience of the resurrection through the gift of the Spirit who is himself both 'first-fruits' (Rom. 8:22-23) and 'pledge' (2 Cor. 5:4-5) of the new Creation. Attention was drawn to this in Chapter V. In both verses we find the tension in Christian existence between the 'already' and the 'not yet'; through God's spirit we have a foretaste of that resurrection as we 'seek those things which are above' (Col. 3:1). The future resurrection impinges upon our present life as we learn to open ourselves to the new life which only God gives.

The second important idea lies in the nature of the resurrection body of the Lord. The New Testament writers saw this as a model of the new nature which each Christian one day will possess. Just as Christ's resurrection body was recognisably himself while it had all the characteristics of a supernatural body, so the Christian will one day inherit that kind of body. Clearly we cannot comprehend the nature of such a body because it is beyond our experience. Yet the clue is there in the resurrection body of Jesus. So John writes, admitting his ignorance of the nature of the resurrection body but certain that Christ's risen nature is the key to Christian hope:

'It does not yet appear what we shall be, but we know that when he appears we shall be like him, for we shall see him as he is' (1 John 3.2).

The resurrection body

With the mention of the resurrection body, modern man shifts uncomfortably and irritably in his seat. 'What on earth do you mean by the resurrection of the body,' he asks, 'when we know so well that our physical body perishes at death?'

The body in this context is not flesh. 'Flesh and blood cannot inherit the Kingdom of Heaven,' says St. Paul (1 Cor. 15:50). The steady assumption of the New Testament in fact is that in heaven the Christian will be 'clothed' with a new body, a spiritual body, fit for eternity and fellowship with God (2 Cor. 5:3). In other words, the concern of the Bible is not with the resuscitation of the body but its resurrection and that is a completely different thing. It is not our physical nature which will be transformed but a new and fitting identity in which the self will be clothed.

This idea of the resurrection is at complete variance with the ancient Greek concept of the immortality of the soul. This latter theory distinguished between a mortal part of man, the body, and its indwelling immortal element, the soul. What happens to the body is of little concern to the soul which, after death, is free of its hindrance. The Biblical emphasis, however, is upon the unity of man as a whole person, not merely a collection of parts. Both Old Testament and New Testament unite in saying firmly 'man *is* a body' and not as the Greeks would say 'man has a body'.

This is consonant with modern thinking. It is impossible to conceive of the personality or the self existing without some bodily expression. In everyday life, thinking, choosing, knowing, loving and other personal experiences involve an experiencing body. What is more, a body is the means whereby we communicate with others. If heaven is a solitary affair, then by all means have your immortal soul. But if heaven is a corporate experience, and this is the clear teaching of the New Testament, then there must be something to take the place of our physical bodies. A body-less soul is, therefore, alien to the Christian faith which insists on some continuity of the person before and after death. This was Thomas Aquinas's point when he insisted, 'my soul is not I; and if souls are saved, I am not saved, nor is any man.'[11]   We must face facts. Modern people *may* find the idea of a resurrection body more comprehensible than that of an immortal soul but this doctrine is not without its difficulties. The two most common problems which we shall consider, are; whether it is possible to talk of a 'self' at all, and whether the physical basis of mental activity destroys belief in the resurrection of the body.

A. The self

As long ago as the eighteenth century David Hume denied the existence of a self, holding it to be illusory. The concept 'I' was, in his opinion, merely a series of disconnected perceptions which created the illusion of a self. So he argues, 'When I enter most intimately into what I call myself, I always stumble on some particular perception or other, I never catch myself at any time without a perception and never can observe anything but perception. What we term 'I', what we cherish and expect to survive, is nothing but a bundle of perceptions.'[12] This seems at first sight to be a powerful argument. Is the self, then, a mirage which has no reality independent of those things which are experienced? Is it like a film made up of thousands of different shots which, when taken at speed, create the illusion of being a whole? According to Hume, therefore, a self does not have experience but is experiences.

When we consider this argument closely, however, we find that its plausibility is not as strong as we first thought. The 'self' is not something one can produce apart from experiences, perceptions, and encounters with others. The self is the basic *me* which is having such experiences, absorbing them, and, yes, even being changed by them and yet still remaining a unique individual. Anyone with children will know how from birth the child, an individual in his own right, is a distinct, continuous self throughout his life. The old man who chuckles reminiscently at the old photo taken of him some seventy years before is totally dissimilar, physically and mentally, from the child in the photo. And yet the identity is there, as others who know him well will tell him, in his character and personality, and this he would acknowledge himself. Furthermore, as Russell Aldwinckle points out, each of us acknowledges this continuous self in daily experience. How convenient it would be, legally and morally, to argue that the person who committed that crime ten years ago was not *me*, because there is no *me* to take the blame. So Aldwinckle observes: 'If the only continuity is a bodily one, what my body did ten years ago is of no concern to me.'[13] We are not saying, as Hume seemed to think his intellectual opponents were saying, that one may strip off the layers of experience until one came at last to a residual self and expose it for all to see. This would lead us back into a false dualism. We must repeat that in the experiences of life the self is known, not created, and it knows itself to be a self-conscious entity, that experiences but is not constituted by experiences. Professor H. D. Lewis, in his brilliant refutation of the materialism of such philosophers as Ryle, Stuart Hampshire and others, calls this irreducible being the 'elusive self' because of the way it eludes our intellectual enquiry while being the basis of such enquiry.[14]

In asserting the existence of the self, mind or soul, whatever term we prefer to use, we are again on a head-on collision course with the views of B. F. Skinner who denies the existence of what he terms 'autonomous man', that is, 'a person who is more than a living body'.[15] The true description of the individual, in Skinner's opinion, is not that of a body with a person inside (whoever said it was?) but an individual, schooled by his environment, displaying a complex 'repertoire of behaviour'. The individual discovers his identity as he learns to distinguish between 'his body' and the rest of the world. The pronouns 'I', 'me', 'he', 'she' and 'you', therefore, are not descriptive terms of independent selves but merely identity labels. Furthermore, if a self is, as Skinner states, a 'repertoire of behaviour appropriate to a given set of contingencies', we are led to the conclusion that one individual can compose two or more selves according to his circumstances. So a person may possess one repertoire appropriate to his family and another in his work. This wholesale reductionism of man to the dominion of his environment leads Skinner to nail his colours very firmly to the mast of deterministic behaviourism: 'Without the help of a verbal community,' he states, 'all behaviour would be unconscious. Consciousness is a social product.'

Two points arise immediately. The first is that Skinner has confused roles with selves. It is self-evident that we play different roles in life. The businessman is a different man at home with his children from what he is in the office. Yet he would find it surprising to be described as two selves. In his view these roles do not contradict each other; both flow from the integrity of his being, and he knows himself to be one person of whose identity he is in no doubt. Even when we play false roles, which we all do from time to time, the normal person is aware of his basic personal identity which accuses him of deception. Secondly, by stating that 'without the help of a verbal community all behaviour would be unconscious', Skinner outlines an extreme view in which man's awareness of himself as an individual comes solely through the environment in which he is set. Such a statement is, of course, impossible to prove or disprove, because we cannot analyse a strictly independent person to find out whether he is a self-conscious human being or not. It is, however, a gross exaggeration to make consciousness a social phenomenon. Society may teach a man to read, write and to reason, but the individual brings to society the raw data of intelligence and individual gifts. Human history is full of evidence of how individuals have transcended society, thus indicating that selves are not society's slaves but creators of society.

In a later book, Skinner's total denial of 'personhood' leads him into a surprising contradiction. On the one hand, 'a person is not an originating agent; he is a locus, a point at which many genetic and environmental conditions come together in a joint effect'. Yet, on the other hand, 'man can now control his own destiny because he knows what must be done and how to do it'.[16] But Skinner cannot have it both ways! Either man is a creature whose behaviour is totally determined by his environment, or 'he can control his own destiny' and must, therefore, be an initiating, creating agent.

B. *Mental processes*

As we have argued, the elusive, 'I' is inextricably linked to the physical and mental processes of the body. I cannot think a thought which is not manifested in chemical activity within that complex computer we call the brain. Of course, this does not mean that we fall into the error of materialism asserting that it is physiological processes which create thought. When I think to myself about a given subject this is not a case of a brain initiating that action but a whole person who is the initiator. We should not be surprised that our thoughts are registered in activity within the brain, and that our emotional lives are regulated by neurological centres within the brain; it is in fact precisely what we should expect if we are psycho-physical beings. Neither is there any serious theological threat from the fact that operations on the brain, such as pre-frontal leucotomy, lobotomy, and even the more drastic hemispher-ectomy, can change human personality for better or worse. If a leucotomy cures a patient of an obsessional neurosis is there any fundamental difference between that operation and a thyroid operation which will also affect the personality of a patient? The patients in both cases are changed, we trust for the better, but identity before and after is maintained. The leucotomy patient, so different now, does not and cannot deny his selfhood; his statement, 'I am better now', indicates this continuity.

But does not the destruction of the brain at death raise serious questions about survival after death? As we have stressed, while we cannot agree with the materialist who makes matter all, we do not step out with the immaterialist who postulates an immaterial 'soul' over and above his physical being. Man is a 'sort of body' to use Peter Geech's phrase,[17] and as we have already concluded personhood is difficult to visualise without some embodiment. The brain shares in the mortality of our flesh and is destined likewise for destruction. This reminds us that it is a false trail to look within the human body for an immortal 'soul', mind, or

residual self which *somehow* survives the destruction of the
flesh. This type of search can end up in desperate straits like
Descartes who believed that the pineal gland housed the soul.
The Bible, however, stresses that eternal life is God's gift to
the Christian. It is not something that is natural to us but it
comes from him; it is not something that comes from within
human nature but from the divine.

We have lingered over this point of the uniqueness of
individuality not only because it is fundamental to Christian
doctrine but also because it affects our whole attitude towards
life. If we are correct about the identity of the self, it is of the
utmost significance for the doctrine of the resurrection of the
body and it ties in most closely with Paul's understanding of
the continuity of the body. In 1 Corinthians 15, dealing with
those who treated the resurrection of the body as a most
unbelievable notion, Paul develops the idea of the common
nature between two apparently different things. 'What you
sow is not the body which is to be, but a bare kernel, perhaps
of wheat or some other grain. But God gives it a body as he
has chosen' (1 Cor. 15:37). There is, we might say, a one-
to-one relationship and continuity between seed and corn
which brackets them together into a unity, however unalike
they look. The same goes for the caterpillar which emerges
from the chrysalis to become a beautiful butterfly. The same
might even hold of Sir John Cutler's famous pair of stockings
which began their life as silk and which by much mending
ended as worsted! So Paul informs us that in the resurrection
the self emerges not as a phantom, a disembodied soul, but an
embodied person. Yet of the nature of that body we will
remain ignorant until it is ours.

There is one element which draws the preceding argument
together. In this volume we have shown how central Jesus is
for the doctrine of man. He is no less significant for man's
future in God. He is the basis for the Christian doctrine of the
resurrection of the dead, being at one and the same time its
harbinger and model. Here we are once more at the centre of
the tension between Jesus as God and man. Both emphases
are crucial for a correct understanding of the resurrection of
all men. Only God after all can raise the dead and, as the
New Testament writers realised, the resurrection of Jesus

declared his real divinity (Acts 2:36; Rom. 1:4). But that, on its own, is cold comfort to mortal man who cannot lay claim to such pedigree. What is *directly* relevant to man is that Jesus steps into man's predicament as man and tastes death for all; 'A second Adam to the fight and to the rescue came.' Perfect obedience is rendered to God even to the point of death (Heb. 5:7-10) and through this unique self-offering and sacrifice life comes to all who turn to him. Here is the difference between this man Christ Jesus and us. In our case life ends in death, a cul-de-sac of fear and hopelessness. But through him life comes from death, an ever-broadening stream of hope and fulfilled destiny,

It is no exaggeration, then, to call Jesus 'paradigm' man not only in terms of human nature generally but also in reference to human destiny. He signals the defeat of death and the prospect of a glorious future for mankind. It is no surprise to learn therefore that the resurrection body which will be ours is one 'like unto his own glorious body' (Phil. 3:21). That is, the present perishable body will be radically transferred into a new spiritual body like that of our Lord's. Paul indeed insists that there is a common identity between the resurrection of Jesus and that of all Christians. What happened to Jesus has bearing on what will happen to us. Immediately after his resurrection he was recognisable as the same Jesus; in the garden, in the upper room and by the lake. Yet, that body so clearly the body of the beloved Jesus was different. This was no 'revived' Jesus but a transformed Jesus with a nature changed to suit a different dimension of living. Now he appears and disappears suddenly (John 20:19); he resists a physical embrace because of this new nature (John 20:17) yet, at the same time that he is no phantom is proved by the fact that he could still eat and drink (Luke 24:43).

Here, then, are clues for that new life in Christ. We see by his experience both the transformation of that human physical body and the continuity between it and the new nature. Our present nature Paul likens to a seed; 'what you sow is not the body which is to be, but a bare kernel, perhaps of wheat or of some other grain' (1 Cor. 15:37). Now the point about a seed is that on its own it is *impossible* to know what kind of flower it will produce. That is why seed distributors very helpfully put a coloured picture of the mature flower on the cover of the seed packet to help us relate seed time to harvest. All we know as Christians is that there is an identity between the 'seed' of our present bodies and the future resurrection. If Christ is the 'representation' of that future in God, then we are content.

Faith, hope and meaning

Christian belief in the survival of the individual after death is not a projection of a selfish immortality-wish, but is only a part of a much greater and important idea, namely the coming of God's Kingdom. God is working his purposes out and will in his good time unite all things in himself (Eph. 2:19-22). In a true sense history is his-story, not in the sense that he is dictating its direction by manipulating human will, but that even through the crass foolishness of men he is working triumphantly. All will end up where he wants it to be. That is why Christian hope is not dismayed or shattered when things happen contrary to human expectation, because the Christian places his trust in God who transcends history. It is true that Christians are often profoundly dismayed when the old order topples and they are left among the rubble with other terrified inhabitants of the earthly city. When this happens it is usually because the true God has been replaced by false gods. The Christian, like the ancient Hebrews, is sometimes tempted to place his trust in the gods of the land. It is easier, after all, to settle for the 'Canaanite' god, localised, stationary and safe — the god of the *status quo* whose job it is to keep things as they are — than the 'nomadic' God of Abraham who is always leading and daily challenging. It is in the majestic nomad-God, or Guide-God as Jurgen Moltmann describes him,[18] that the Christian must put his trust; the one who leads his people through the dangerous and difficult wilderness to the Promised Land. Like Moses, it is his back we see (Exod. 33:23).

While the distinctive hope of the Christian is based on the work and promises of Christ, mankind as a whole knows the value of hope and the inspiration it brings. It is no exaggeration to say that all human progress has been inspired by hope.

Hope drove Christopher Columbus westwards and hope was the magnet which drew the early American settlers into the unconquered territories of the wild west. Hope continues to be the spring of human activity, sacred and secular. Man cannot live without hope. If there is no tomorrow, today is flat and meaningless.

If it is true that man cannot live fruitfully and purposefully without hope, the question of importance for modern man is: What is the effect upon man when he loses hope in God and hope of a life beyond the grave?

First of all, disbelief in eternal things affects the quality of man's present existence and his deepest values. Some would argue to the contrary, that the ready acceptance that this life is all frees man to find fulfilment in his present existence unencumbered by the fears and fantasies of a spiritual utopia or doom. But is this really so? Nietzsche, the so-called assassin of God, did not believe so. He saw the significance of the loss of hope and realised the profound repercussions it had upon all values. He was deeply affected by the conviction that God was dead. This was the most terrible and world-shattering discovery and brought him unbearable loneliness. It necessitated, furthermore, the transvaluation of all values, for if God is dead nothing can be true and everything is permissible. Indeed, he poured contempt on the English who rejected the Christian faith but kept Christian standards and values;[19] as he saw correctly, they belong together. Dietrich Bonhoeffer, writing his momentous work on ethics in Hitler's Germany, dominated as it was by Nietzschean ideology, saw clearly that the rejection of life hereafter did not lead to an idolisation of life but an idolisation of death. He writes:

> Where death is the first thing, earthly life is all or nothing. Boastful reliance on earthly eternities goes side by side with a frivolous playing with life. A convulsive acceptance and seizing hold of life stands cheek by jowl with indifference and contempt for life. There is no clearer indication of the idolisation of death than when a period claims to be building for eternity and yet life has no value in this period, or when big words are spoken of a new man, of a new world, and of a new society which is to be ushered in,

and yet all that is new is the destruction of life as we have it.[20]

No doubt good people will always be good, and bad people bad, in spite of the possibility of heaven or hell, but there can be little doubt that eternity, the assurance of a life beyond, gives significance for human activity here and now. If death is the end, then every human enterprise is clouded and all ends in ultimate futility; all, in the words of Ecclesiastes, is a 'striving after wind' (Eccles. 2:17). Denial of immortality will not make life more precious and important, as Bonhoeffer saw. On the contrary, the earthly life takes on the hue of having little human significance and value. If this life is all, this fact will dominate the thinking person's activity and life-style; sacrifice for others, though highly estimable, will hardly be logical, since all is basically meaningless and all plunge into the same pitiless dark void of eternal death. Self-love becomes the only logical stance in such an indifferent universe. This conclusion may be deplorable but it is irresistible. Where God is not, not even man is all, but nihilism and despair prevail.

Many people today, however, evade the frightening consequences of a world without God by the subterfuge of transferring their attention to temporal hopes. At the ordinary level these hopes are as basic as the next pay rise, next year's holiday, leisure activities or the ambition for a higher standard of living. There is also a deeper level in which man hopes for a better future, a heaven on earth, and even the limitless progress of mankind whose inheritance is the planets. But we do not need a prophet to tell us that secular eschatologies have failed. The world is faced by vast problems undreamed of a few decades ago. An exhausted nature, squeezed dry by man's thoughtless greed, overpopulated and misused, offers little comfort for generations to come. The secular future is bleak, with the result that secular Utopias have been replaced by temporal expedients. Few ecologists are confident about the long-term future of mankind on this planet. Alvin Toffler reports that many young American radicals share a common 'disbelief in the future' and find themselves incapable of 'formulating the future.'[21]

The Golden Age is over because the goose which laid the golden eggs is now barren. We have yet to see whether man, without hope and without God in this world, can cope as the night closes in around him.

In this situation the Christian body is called to a threefold task.

First of all, it must reaffirm its commitment to eternal realities. The Church, influenced overmuch by secular thinking, has become too embarrassed to speak clearly of heaven, limiting such utterances to credal and doctrinal statements. Sermons and talks on issues in eschatology are rare indeed in Christian congregations with the accent very much on living in the present. Of course we have no adequate conception of heaven, and often we feel that explanations have to be edged with so many qualifications that silence is the best policy. But this is the way of cowardice. What is required today is not a de-mythologising of language but a *re*-mythologising of language in modern terms to convey to people the meaningfulness of the Christian hope. Although we cannot talk about 'streets of solid gold', yet we can talk, as the Book of Revelation does, in confident terms of relationships with Christ and to one another in the world to come; the triumph of God's Kingdom; the coming of a new order in which justice, love, peace and harmony will govern all things. Unless the Church is prepared to speak with conviction, confidence, and boldness about heavenly things it will continue in failing to address the needs of the modern world.

The second task confronting Christian people is to challenge the secular and materialistic values of our society and to question whether it is wise to place all our eggs in earthly baskets. Utopia on earth is an impossible ideal, and Christianity will have none of it. We believe, not in the transformation of today into a better tomorrow, but in the death of the old and the birth of a new heaven and earth. This does not mean that the Christian must opt out of the present and ignore what he doesn't agree with. He is committed to the provisional and he must work for a better tomorrow, but at the same time he knows that the provisional has to give way eventually to God's Kingdom.

Thirdly, and perhaps most boldly of all, the Church is

challenged to represent the destiny of redeemed mankind. The idea of the Church as an outpost of heaven may be almost laughable to those who are only too keenly aware of its weaknesses and sin, but this idea is not without some biblical warrant. Paul for instance could speak of the tiny Philippian Church as a 'colony of heaven', shining like a star for God in the darkness of the world (Phil. 2:14-16). The Church must increasingly recognise its role as an eschatological community living in hope and expectation of the coming of the Kingdom. Not only waiting, but working; working, praying and living for that goal which is not a man-made utopia but a Christ-made destiny in which God himself becomes the true goal and end of man.

NOTES

1   B. F. Skinner, *Beyond Freedom and Dignity*, p. 210.
2   Pascal, *Pensées*, 206.
3   Malinowski, *Sex, Culture and Myth* (Rupert Hart-Davis, 1963), p. 263-264.
4   *Ethics*, 1115a, 11.
5   *Fragment*, XLVII.
6   *Antigone*, V. 332, 360.
7   *Meditations*, IV, 21; VI, 13.
8   Quoted by J. Choron, *Death in Western Thought* (Collier, N.Y., 1963), p. 232.
9   J. Choron, *op. cit.*, p. 118.
10 *Jesus, God and Man*, (SCM, 1968), p. 109.
11 Commentary on 1 Cor. 15.
12 *A Treatise of Human Nature*, 4. 6. 4.
13 *Death in the Secular City* (Allen and Unwin, 1972), p. 78.
14 H. D. Lewis, *The Elusive Mind* (Allen and Unwin, 1969), see also G. Vesey, *Personal Identity* (Macmillan, 1974), for a brilliant examination of Hume's argument concerning 'perception'.
15 *Beyond Freedom and Dignity*, p. 192.
16 *About Behaviourism* (Cape, 1975).
17 P. Geech, *God and the Soul*, p. 26.
18 *A Theology of Hope* (SCM, 1967), p. 162.
19 *Twilight of the Idols* (Penguin Classic, 1968).
20 D. Bonhoeffer, *Ethics*, p. 78.
21 *Future Shock* (Bantam Books, 1970), ch. 20.

CHAPTER 9

Open to God

I Believe in Man is the title of this book. It stands to reason that such a confessional title can only describe one man's way of looking at life and mankind. In this volume I have given my interpretation of the Christian teaching about man, making no claims for infallibility or comprehensiveness. It is my hope, however, that what I have written may help others arrive at a better understanding of Christian teaching, as well as inspiring a greater confidence in it.

Man, as I have described him, lives in the intersection of two spheres. He is a natural and physical being, but one who no less definitely dwells within the indefinable spiritual realm. His problems begin when he tries to deny one or other of these spheres, or when he distorts their relationship. But he is, in addition, a creature of contradictions. Called by God to high responsibilities and dignity within creation, and equipped at the same time with intellect and moral judgment to carry this programme out, his performance is no more than a pale shadow of his promise. His capacity for the highest standards of integrity and self-sacrifice is outstripped by his capacity for self-destruction and cruelty. The Biblical story of man's 'progress' is in one sense a sad saga of his longing to escape all he loathes in his nature. Alas! Failure stalks every attempt. There is, says the Bible, a tragedy in the heart of man — what he loathes, he loves; what he wants to relinquish, he clings to. But scripture makes an equally bold claim; that the riddle of man is only solved through God's intervention into human life. Only Christ, the Christian faith proclaims, is the key to life and freedom; only he can satisfy man's hunger and longing.

Such a world-view contrasts sharply with secular perspectives, several of which we have considered in this volume. Whatever these viewpoints and however disparate they may be, they agree on one thing — that the claims of Christianity are quite laughable and meaningless today. Old Mother Church, cuddling tightly its precious mythology behind its stained glass windows, has little to say to modern man who, through his conquest of his environment, is lord of all.

It is important to emphasise again that the Christian does not disparage all the insights given by secular world-views. He is grateful for all he has learned and will continue to learn. But it is manifestly clear from man's recent history that the divinity conferred upon him is a little premature. The expectation of man's inevitable and unhurried advance towards peace and prosperity has been shattered by the vast problems which now face him. 'The future of our earth now lies in the hands of man,' trumpeted Julian Huxley as recently as 1959.[1] But man's handling of such problems as poverty, overpopulation, war, unemployment, to name but a few, has not inspired confidence in his ability to control the world's future on his own.

Ironically, alongside scientific research which engendered such earlier self-assurance in man's nature and ability, specialist studies have emerged which tell him another story; a story of his smallness, insignificance and fate. So genetics tells him that he is a biological accident; anthropology describes him as an ape under his fashionable dress; literature portrays neurosis as his present hazard; history informs him that he is decadent; philosophy pronounces him meaningless; and sociology diagnoses his current disease as 'anomie'.

It is easy, of course, to exaggerate the problems facing mankind and the despair in his heart. After all, millions of our contemporaries lead, as far as we can tell, contented lives unconcerned by the doom pronounced upon them. But the fact remains that the myth of 'superman', the basis of many secular views, has been dealt a death blow by events. Man may have become quite expert at manipulating his environment, but he is a long way from adequate government of himself. This 'Achilles heel' makes him a danger to himself and his society. General Omar Bradley expressed the power and weakness of man in this way: 'Our knowledge of science has clearly outstripped our capacity to control it. We have too many men of science, too few men of God. We have grasped the mystery of the atom and rejected the Sermon on the Mount. Man is stumbling through a spiritual darkness while toying with the secrets of life and earth...ours is a world of nuclear giants and ethical infants.' To put it another way, man the technologist is all-powerful while man the technician is sick, and as long as that sickness is undiagnosed and untreated, he is a danger to all.

If then we should accept genuine insights about man brought to our attention by modern knowledge, we must seek to discover in return those Christian insights that bear upon modern secular life.

The mistake of traditional Christianity has lain in its presentation of man as a finished being destined for God. We have been too content with old-fashioned categories, with the result that a great gulf has grown between Christian thought and the modern world. Christians are beginning to see that repetition of old slogans does not constitute truth or necessarily carry conviction; instead ideas must be translated into modern terms and take into account fresh thought and knowledge. On the other hand, the mistake of secular points of view has lain in their choice of unworthy models to define man. Some thinkers have tried to interpret humanity in the light of animal behaviour. To some extent this is legitimate. Man is a natural being and, therefore, helpful parallels may be found between human civilisation and animal environment. But the 'animal' model breaks down before the complexity and distinctiveness of man; it fails to take into account his mental superiority and moral ascendancy. Others have sought a definition in the 'machine' model. There are striking parallels here also. Man is an intricate 'mechanism' capable of giving good 'results'; his brain is a complex computor, although only one tenth is actually utilised; he is, furthermore, a machine which malfunctions occasionally and experts are called in to deal with the faulty parts. But press the analogy too far and we end up de-personalising a creature who transcends such definitions.

It is with the 'person' model that Christianity makes its most distinctive contribution. What is a 'person'? We usually define personhood by three characteristics. These three ways will show clearly why such categories as 'animal' or 'machine' are inadequate descriptions of mankind. Firstly, a person is a responsible being; he is self motivated and free to choose. It is obvious that accountability is never expected of machines or animals. Secondly, a person is capable of loving. By this we mean more than an emotional attachment, we mean the unconditional giving up of oneself to another, for the other's sake and not one's own. This 'irrationality' is most un-machinelike; it cannot be programmed, or accounted for on any other basis than that we regard others as priceless beings. Thirdly, a person needs something to live for. Animals can live without meaning, and machines do not ask *why* they are made, but persons do. Persons know what purpose is, what objectives mean, what ideals are for and how important they are for human life.

Such descriptions of man *as* an animal or man *as* a machine are helpful approximations but feeble definitions. Man *is* a person and surpasses such analogies by reason of his creativity and response to life. Central to this creativity is man's openness to all things. Only man can reach out within his environment and beyond it, and, in his openness to all reality, we find further intimations of his nature as a spiritual being. Let us consider three areas in which man reaches out beyond himself.

Openness to the World

We noted in Chapter 1 that the debate still continues concerning the difference between man and other creatures. One obvious fact, however, is that whereas other beings are more or less fixed in their final form, man is an 'emergent' being. 'Man is unique,' said Julian Huxley, 'in being the only type of organism capable of anything big in the way of further development.'[2] Overcoming his physical limitations he creates civilisations and cultures for himself. But such 'openness' is never merely a means to an end. No sooner is that civilisation or culture completed than he is building bigger and better forms to satisy his desires.

Is there anything significant about man's drive in this way? The important element lies in the unsatisfied nature of his quest for a world beyond himself. No sooner is one thing completed than he is leaving it for another. He has an insatiable curiosity to know and be known. Yet in this quest for fulfilment, for knowledge, for possession, lies the paradox of humanity — his needs always lie beyond anything he can attain in the way of material goods. In a typical aphorism Pascal sums up man's quest for things above and beyond him: 'Man infinitely surpasses man.'[3] It is not surprising, then, that man's openness to life makes it necessary for him to develop spiritual cultures alongside the material forms as sustenance for his deeper nature. 'Man does not live by bread alone' is true of human beings at any time. He is driven by his spiritual needs to grope beyond material things to God. A result of this side of his personality is that only man poses deep and searching questions about life, death, meaning and so on. These we may call 'God-questions' because they examine the meaning of ultimate things.

Openness to moral demands

An element within man's openness to the world is an awareness that the demands made by others cannot easily be avoided or denied. Try as we may to shrug off our obligations to others, we know of demands within us which call for obedience. Imperatives which begin with the formula 'thou shalt' or 'thou shalt not' are not out-of-date ethics which come from an obscure eastern hill nearly three millenna ago, but part of the framework of man's humanity. For example, is it wrong to kill? The chorus of affirmation which comes from the different cultures and societies of mankind is that to kill wantonly and cruelly *is* wrong. The Nuremberg trial was a demonstration of the world's conviction that Hitler's deeds against the Jews were evils perpetrated against humanity itself. Though the Nazis could claim that they were acting in accord with the constitution of the country and in line with social and political planning, they stood condemned by a

higher law. To a considerable extent, we all *know* what is right
and wrong. This is true of the individual as well as the group.
In things relating to property, relationships, and respect for
the dignity and honour of others — to name but few of our
obligations — we are conscious that as individuals we are not
the sole reference point, but that others confront us as beings
with rights.

But the problem about morality is that if it is external to
us, its objectivity is different from, say, that of the book before
us. The command 'thou shalt love thy neighbour as thyself'
is not self-evident and not easy to justify if man is all alone in
the universe. Rex Warner outlines the same problem but
from a different perspective: 'Many have fought against
fascism in the belief that each individual has a unique value
and that no state or organisation of men should be permitted
to override or crush what is each man's uniqueness, his
personality; yet this is a belief which, in the past, has rested
on the belief in God for whom every soul is valuable and,
without the belief in God, the strange paradox, so contrary to
the trend of events, that the individual is uniquely important
is, to say the least, not easy to justify.'[4] Indeed it is not; but
the fact is that moral obligations thrust themselves upon us in
the bustle of daily living. And equally apparent, to destroy
the framework of morality, to relativise it away, is to attack
the nature of humanity. Even if we believed with Huxley that
man will control and direct the future evolution of our
planet, it is as a moral and responsible being that we (and
Huxley) would wish him to exercise that role.

Many thinkers have seen with Warner that in the moral
direction of man's life a strong argument for the existence of
God can be made. Be that as it may, the point we are making
is that in moral demands we are aware of ourselves as
spiritual beings. When we search our motives and ask *why* we
act in these ways and what justification we have for acting
honourably, nobly, or sacrificially we might find that the
most satisfactory answer comes when we include God in the
context. Openness to others is seen by Christians as a form of
openness to God, in that he is the validity for moral action
and growth.

Openness to God

It is often admitted by non-Christians today that at the centre of the problem of man there is a spiritual malaise. Colin Wilson quotes Shaw with approval that 'civilisation cannot exist without a religion'.[5] Such writers, nevertheless, are careful to point out that *ersatz* scientific religions will do equally well. But the fact is that such alternatives just will *not* do, because it is essential for any faith that it is believed for its own sake. The moment it is recognised as a laboratory-made panacea to account for the 'meaninglessness' of life or to bolster up a civilisation, its plausibility is at an end.

What has caused this malaise? For some, the intellectual problems of faith present the greatest obstacles. Such problems are many and varied; they range from such questions about the nature of the universe and the problem of pain, to the failure and ineffectiveness of the Church. With such questions Christians must continue to wrestle, showing the reasonableness of faith and the integrity of the gospel. But there are also sociological reasons why men do not believe. We have to face the fact that materialism and secularism make it very difficult for modern people to consider Christianity honestly, openly and freely. Christian truth, these days, is often greeted by deep prejudice, contempt or polite indifference. The odds are stacked against free enquiry into spiritual realities because materialism is rampant. But a further reason lies in man's avoidance of God. 'Adam, where are you?' is a question not just addressed to Adam in the Genesis story but God's call to each and every one of us. Like Adam, many people today prefer to stay 'closed' to God.

Whether people cannot believe, or are conditioned not to believe, or will simply not believe, man is by nature potentially open to God and this element is the thing that makes him distinctively human. This is, admittedly, a controversial statement, but one to which I stick unreservedly. What makes a man human is not his abnormal brain, his language ability, or his creativity; but the fact that, when all is said and done, he is a spiritual being. Although it is often said that millions of people get on quite well without any great pretensions to religious belief, this is not relevant at all.

Many of our contemporaries, after all, have a subliminal or an untaught faith, while the rootlessness and restlessness of others is really a quest for faith. 'Our hearts are restless until they rest in thee' is true of the twentieth-century American, German or Englishman just as it was of the fourth century Augustine.

How many people become open to God? I once knew a man who, because of his fixation about finding lost coins and valuables, never raised his eyes off the ground; he found many coins, indeed, but what he lost in failing to appreciate the beauty of the world and the glory of life is incalculable. Similarly, we in our materialistic society have lost the sense of wonder at the glories of creation. We are accustomed to think of things as utility objects to be consumed, used, dissected, or documented. Rarely do we consider them as objects to admire, to be treated in their own right. It will be as man realises his 'oneness' with the world and learns to reflect, richly, deeply, upon this amazing, vast, awesome universe of which he is part, that he will become open to his Creator.

Equally, man must wonder at himself instead of belittling his nature and purpose. Who is this creature that laments a 'dead' God and chides the universe for making him an orphan? Such a fretful conclusion ends up by dismissing life itself as futility, man as a joke, and death as the only rational element because it ends the nightmare. Who is this creature, anyhow, who poses the riddle and sees himself as a 'useless passion'? Even now, his space rockets interview the planets millions of miles away; his heroism and sacrifice contradict the worthlessness he claims he is; and his undoubted ability in science, literature, art and religion deny his peevish attempts to be a meaningless speck of cosmic dust. Man may be a mystery to himself, but he is also a source of wonder. As he contemplates this aspect he is led away from himself into the nearness and greater wonder of God who has bequeathed to man such dignity.

It must be clearly understood that until man realises his need of God such openness can never become a channel for God and man to meet. Our wretchedness, unworthiness, and knowledge of our spiritual need induce us to seek God and prove the existence of God far more effectively than any

argument. Here, in the area of human helplessness without
God, we arrive at a knowledge of our infinite yet unfulfilled
capacity to enter into a loving relationship with him. Such a
relationship once begun is never completely explored in this
life but exists as a draw to something far deeper, higher and
exciting than we have yet found.

The statement 'I believe in man' thus requires us to believe
certain things about God and his relationship with mankind.
The Christian will want to put it, 'I believe in man because I
first believe in God.' Without God man is nothing; with God
he is a being of dignity and honour because he is made in
God's image and destined for wonderful things. Pico della
Mirandola, a Renaissance writer, makes God say to man:

> I have put thee in the centre of the universe in order for
> thee to see better what is there. I did not make thee either a
> heavenly or earthly creature, either mortal or immortal. I
> created thee so that as thine own sculptor thou makest
> thine own features. Thou canst degenerate into an animal,
> but thou canst also be reborn, through the freewill of thy
> spirit, into the image of God.[6]

Such then is man's potential; with God everything is his,
without God there is nothing of eternal value. The importance of the individual and the worthwhileness of human
existence are bound up with the nature and goodness of God
who confers on man his blessings. Naturally, in our more
cynical moments we may question whether man's performance will ever rise to the promise of his nature and destiny.
As with Concorde, we might wonder equally of man 'will the
staggering cost ever be repaid or redeemed?' It is proper to
ask such a question; but it is not for us to answer it. Only the
Creator is entitled to reply, and he himself has given his
answer in his self-giving love in Christ. That love, expressed
in such a surprising and staggering way, is quite beyond our
understanding, and yet it discloses the transcendent mercy of
God. God's love in Christ — his estimate of what we are
worth — gives us all the confidence we need to live truly,
fearlessly, in full humanity.

It is fitting that Jesus, God's man, should end this book

about man. As 'true' man he calls mankind to himself, to experience the newness and the fullness of life which he offers. But he also challenges those who know him to reaffirm him before others as the hope and goal of the human race.

As we look into the future, no one really knows what road humanity will take, beset as it is by vást problems such as it has never faced before. Without God, the future of man is very bleak indeed, but in Christ the promise is already given to man. God, who said 'let us make man in our own image', remakes man at Calvary. In the light of that cross and resurrection we can be confident that there is a destiny for man. Through Christ alone will Tennyson's dream materialise:

All about him shadow still, but,
while the races flower and fade,
Prophet-eyes may catch a glory slowly gaining on the shade.
Till the peoples all are one,
and all their voices blend in choric
Hallelujah to the Maker, It is finished.
Man is made[7]

NOTES

1   Julian Huxley (Ed.), *The Destiny of Man* (Hodder & Stoughton, 1959), p. 19.
2   *The Destiny of Man*, p. 19.
3   *Pensées* (Penguin Classics), p. 66.
4   R. Warner, *The Cult of Power and other Essays* (Bodley Head, 1946), chapter entitled 'May 1945'.
5   C. Wilson, *Beyond the Outsider* (Pan Books, 1965), p. 181.
6   Pico della Mirandola, *Oration on the Dignity of Man* (Quoted in J. Choron, *Death and Western Thought*).
7   Alfred Tennyson, *Poetical Works*, (Oxford Univ. Press, 1953), 'The Meaning of Man', p. 827.

Index